Migrant Soul

The Story of an American Convert

Rabbi Avi Shafran

Migrant Soul
The Story of an American Ger

First published 1992
Copyright © 2012 by Avi Shafran
ISBN-13: 978-1478215233
ISBN-10: 1478215232

Published by:
Hashgacha Press
12 Roanoke St.
Staten Island, N.Y. 10314

Contents

There are two ways to become part of the Jewish people.
One is the path Ovadyah Gomes took.
The other is being born to a Jewish mother.
This book is dedicated to the memory of Rebbetzin Puah Shafran,
my mother and teacher,
who gave me my own Jewish identity in more ways than one
and who remains a shining example of a life
beautifully, meaningfully, Jewishly lived.

In Gratitude

I don't know how to adequately thank Ovadyah and Ariella Gomes for allowing me to intrude upon their lives. It was almost a year after I approached Ovadyah about this project that he finally acquiesced to it. It was not a decision he or his wife took lightly; they relented only because of the good I convinced them might come of this book.

While the bulk of the countless hours of interviews I conducted were spent with them, I owe a substantial debt of gratitude as well to all the others who agreed to interviews and shared their homes and recollections with me.

My deep thanks, too, to the entire staff of Targum Press for their encouragement, constructive criticism and efficiency, and especially to Tzvi Shapiro, my editor, for his always helpful comments, criticisms and suggestions.

Above all, though, my greatest debt in this project, as in so many things in my life, is to my wife, Gita. It was no easy task for her to juggle her many and constant responsibilities to our family and to others with serving as my proofreader and first editor. Her corrections (in life as well as in writing), suggestions and boundless encouragement have exemplified the sublime nature of a true partner in life.

A Message from the Publisher

When Ovadyah Gomes decided to become a Jew, he had no idea of how many halachic issues would arise. Critical questions dealing with the laws of conversion and family life were eventually posed by Ovadyah and his wife, Ariella, to recognized Torah authorities. The issues they faced, and the answers and guidance they received, are faithfully and sensitively recorded in Migrant Soul. The reader is cautioned, however, that these issues are complex and very often depend on individual circumstances. Therefore, this book cannot be used as a halachic guide. Any questions of this nature must be referred to a competent *halachic* authority.

A Note on Veracity

Migrant Soul is based on the lives of Ovadyah and Ariella Gomes, though those are not their real names.

While a modicum of imagination was employed in reconstructing the time, place and details of incidents and conversations, everything described here actually occurred.

Likewise, all the characters in *Migrant Soul* are based on real people, though most names have been changed. Certain characters, moreover, are composites of more than one individual, so no real person should be seen as the absolute model for any character herein, and any resemblance between a character in this book and any actual person, living or dead, should be regarded as coincidental.

Introduction

Having been invited to the Rosens' for a Rosh HaShanah meal, my wife, Gita, and I knew we would not be their only guests. Ron and Dina Rosen always seemed to be hosting others in their home, near-strangers as likely as close friends. Themselves *baalei teshuvah*, or "returnees" to Jewish tradition — though having long since made the transition to a wholly Orthodox lifestyle — the Rosens were always especially anxious to share their lives with anyone they felt might benefit spiritually from seeing Jewish observance up close.

The New England city in which we lived at the time was, at least with respect to Jewish life, well beyond a small town, yet far indeed from a metropolis. Several small Orthodox congregations functioned in town, though only two could accurately have been described as quicker than comatose. A few well-endowed Conservative and Reform congregations rounded out the picture of local Jewish life.

As we strolled back from shul, Gita remarked, and I concurred, how nice it was that the Rosens had taken us and our five small children on for a meal. They had insisted we bring the entire family. And our suspicion that our hosts had not limited their guest list to our family for this holiday meal was confirmed soon enough.

Just as we reached their house, we saw the Rosens arriving from the city's other Orthodox minyan. With them were two adults and two nine-year-old twin girls. The twins were striking beyond the mere cuteness of pre-adolescent girls. There was a special, nebulous charm about them. The word "modest" came to mind, for they were unusually quiet and well-behaved and carried themselves like much older young ladies. But the word did no justice to their demeanor. Something else seemed to emanate from their endearing, entirely identical smiles. We smiled back, though our smiles were no match for theirs, and then looked up at their parents as Dina introduced us.

The mother was a stately, handsome woman who seemed in her middle thirties. She was fair-skinned, with determined, intelligent and penetrating eyes. Inches beneath them, a polite smile articulated the requisite pleasantries.

Her husband exuded what in Yiddish goes by the word "*eidelkeit*," an amalgam of nobility, kindness and grace. He, too, smiled — a wide, warm and irresistible smile. His features were pleasant and well-proportioned, and he wore a dark suit on his trim frame and a colored *kippah* on his head. He seemed about his wife's age (though he was, as we later found out, several years younger), and other than his milk-chocolate complexion and subtly exotic features, there was nothing outwardly remarkable about the man who had just wished us "*Gut Yomtov*" and was introduced as Ovadyah Gomes.

His wife's name was Ariella, and the girls were identified as Ruth and Daphna.

Ron, to whom openness was a high ideal, continued his introduction with the observation that Ovadyah belonged to Beth Am, the largest Conservative congregation in the city, and that he had not been born Jewish, but had been converted by that synagogue's rabbi, Franklin J. Shoman. Implicit in Ron's words was the fact that Ovadyah's conversion was, to Orthodox Jews like Ron, Dina, Gita and me, no conversion at all.

As it happened, Ovadyah himself was well aware of that fact, as I suspected even then and very soon confirmed. Indeed, within hours, I would learn that not only was this dark-skinned man aware of his status in Orthodoxy, but he bore nothing in common with the all-too-typical Conservative or Reform convert. This was no gentile fiancé seeking acceptance from prospective Jewish in-laws, no armchair Judeophile casually seeking to add affiliation to affection. Ovadyah was something entirely different, and he acknowledged the addendum to his introduction with quiet comprehension in his eyes and a grace I would come to know well in his smile.
Jewish or not, he was a pleasure to meet.

The meal was lovely, the unbroken rule for meals at the Rosens', and our conversation spanned a wide range of topics. The meaning of Rosh HaShanah occupied us at the outset; we discussed the idea of temporal "beginnings" in Judaism, and how they so potently determine the character of what follows. We spoke about the problems and joys of raising children, as our own and the Gomeses' joined the Rosens' and together transformed the adjacent living-room area into a playroom carpeted with toys. But what we spoke of most was the "pluralistic" state of the modern Jewish experience.

Ovadyah and Ariella were full of questions — and good ones.

"Why does Orthodoxy claim the only authentic interpretation of Jewish law? Isn't the Talmud full of differing approaches to all sorts of legal issues?" Ariella asked, starting the pinball rolling. "Well, there's actually a fundamental difference," I began, hoping I wouldn't lose these endearing new friends so soon. "The very bedrock of the Talmudic system is the Divinity of Torah as given at Sinai in the ultimate revelation of God to man. The Talmudic rabbis argued not over what *they* felt the law should be, but over what God's will is for us. The Conservative movement doesn't even insist on a belief in the Sinaic revelation, much less an ultimate concern for its demands on us."

"But it does," injected Ovadyah. "It claims no less a concern with tradition than Orthodoxy does. It has a halachic process, complete with scholars who consult the traditional texts when deciding legal questions."

"Does it really, though?" I interrupted. "Is the Conservative movement really concerned with what the Torah wants from us, or with what it wants from the Torah? Is its 'halachic process' an objective, honest one, or a sham? I'll tell you one thing, it's as predictable as fireworks on the Fourth of July."

"What do you mean?"

One of my many faults is trying to claim more than my proper allotment in conversation, which is, after all, supposed to be a two-sided business. Unfortunately for our new acquaintances, I wasn't out of character that afternoon.

"Let me tell you a true story about my teacher and mentor, Rabbi Yaakov Weinberg, may he live and be well, who is a prophet."

Puzzled looks all around, as I had expected.

"In the mid-'70s, Rabbi Weinberg predicted that the president of the Mormon Church would soon receive a `Divine' directive to abolish the ban on black priests. He claimed that, without a doubt, the Elder would hear from `Above' that blacks were now welcome in the priesthood. And in 1978, that's exactly what happened. Spencer Kimball heard from `God' that the previously `accursed' race was suddenly in every way acceptable."

What Rabbi Weinberg was saying, I explained, was that religions which are essentially opportunistic will be embarrassingly predictable when it comes to their legal rulings. Nearly two decades of successful struggle for civil rights was a fact the Mormons simply could not ignore. They suddenly found their religion hopelessly outdated and, in the emerging public mind, quite ugly. The only solution was for their god to "change his mind," which was, conveniently, just what happened.

"The picture is not terribly different," I continued, "when you look at the Conservative record. When, for example, the agitation for what our society calls `equality' for women became unbearable, the Conservative leadership resolved not to be left `behind the times,' lest it erode the movement's entire attraction. Instead, it allowed women to play roles that Halachah has always clearly considered those of men alone. The `halachic' justification, such as it was, came only afterward, as a way of legitimizing what had all along been a foregone conclusion. That's not man seeking God's will; that's man using God to further his own."

Another of my faults, one no less evident that afternoon, is pontificating. The Gomeses were generous, though; they ignored any excesses of mine and seemed concerned only with the argument at hand.

"Do you mean to say," Ovadyah asked quietly, without the slightest hint of offense at my soliloquy, "that Orthodoxy doesn't take the social milieu into account? That the realities of the modern world are of no concern to Halachah?"

I took a deep breath. These people, bless 'em, weren't interested in the usual line-drawing in the sand; they actually wanted to *understand*.

I proceeded to describe the subtle but critical difference between factoring reality into a halachic equation, and seeing Halachah as a mere game to be played before granting automatic legitimacy to every passing societal fancy. The first approach was "God-centered"; the second, "man-centered."

Ariella asked, earnestly and without defensiveness, why Orthodoxy wouldn't recognize a Conservative conversion that included all the requisite halachic elements. At this point, I was forced to introduce the subject of standards for witnesses, a decisive factor in, among many other things, the halachah of conversion.

"Can affiliates of a movement that does not even demand acceptance of the millennia-old bases of Judaism actually be considered candidates for the role of `witness,' a role with clear and stringent requirements, including full acceptance of Jewish belief?"

That led us into a digression about exactly what constitutes Jewish belief, and about the historicity of the revelation at Sinai and the immutability of the halachic process.

Then Ovadyah posed the next thoughtful question.

"Well, what about a Conservative rabbi and Conservative witnesses who *have* accepted all that Orthodoxy considers fundamental to Jewish belief? Would their conversion procedure be accepted by Orthodoxy?"

I think I danced around that complex question by raising a different but equally critical one: the question of the potential convert's acceptance of the entirety of Jewish law. Since such acceptance is a clear requirement of the conversion process according to Orthodoxy, could a candidate for conversion whose idea of Judaism is something other than the traditional one be considered to have accepted, even in principle, the demands of Judaism?

The discussion continued in that direction and everyone contributed to the calm but determined dialectic.

Though Dina is a superb cook, I have not the slightest recollection of what we ate.

The children eventually became restless, and while neither of the Rosens had indicated anything of the sort, I felt we had imposed on their graciousness quite enough for one afternoon. So Gita and I gathered up our family and bid everyone a happy holiday and a year of blessing.

Only as we walked home did we realize how intense the discussion had been and how exhausted we both were. When we reached our house, we put the smaller children to bed for a nap and sent the others into the yard to play. Gita relaxed on the couch and I fell into the recliner.

We weren't home more than a half-hour when a knock on the front door announced a visitor.

I got up, opened the door, and was momentarily disoriented to see Ovadyah and Ariella before me. Their daughters had joined our children in the yard and Ovadyah, still smiling, still intent, spoke.

"Could you re-explain the *Kuzari*'s argument for the acceptance of Sinai as a historical fact?"

I had certainly suspected as much before, but at that moment I knew without a doubt that these were very, very special people.

This, for the benefit of all who have not been privileged to know them, is their story.

Prologue

Divine Providence

The fifteenth century on the Iberian peninsula was a time of explosive discovery. No longer shackled by the weighty chains of the human imagination, distant lands were, for the first time, described by men who had actually seen and touched them.

The pioneering navigational power was the kingdom of Portugal. Inspired at first by Prince Henry, who had earned the epithet "The Navigator," and later by King John II, Portuguese explorers laid claim to the coastal areas of Africa, India and the Malay peninsula, eventually dominating sea routes as far away as the South China Sea. When Spain entered the realm of nautical empire-building, the Portuguese, sensing the need to keep things orderly, negotiated the Treaty of Tordesillas in 1494, dividing the world between the two powers with an imaginary longitudinal line far off the west coast of Africa. All lands discovered to the west of the meridian would belong to Spain, and all those to the east, to Portugal.

Traveling east from that imaginary line in the Atlantic Ocean, one approaches Africa. But the first dry land one encounters is a group of islands about four hundred miles west of modern-day Senegal. These uninhabited islands were named for the verdant African promontory that lay east, in Portuguese *Capo Verde*. They are still known today as the Cape Verde Islands.

The islands quickly became a supply station for ships and a transit point for the Atlantic slave trade. As Portuguese nationals settled the area, refugees from countless foreign lands washed up on the newly discovered shores, and the population of the Cape Verde Islands began to acquire the racial variety it exhibits to this day.

Toward the end of the Portuguese and Spanish expansion of the civilized world, yet another voyager set off from the Iberian peninsula. This Genoese sailor went west, the opposite direction of the ships that had discovered the Cape Verde Islands and Africa beyond. Interestingly, his ship's log begins with a reference to an edict evicting professed Jews from the land that receded behind him. It read, in part:

In the same month in which their Majesties issued the edict that all Jews should be driven out of the kingdom and its territories, in the same month they gave me the order to undertake with sufficient men my expedition of discovery to the Indies.

Cristoforo Colombo, to us Christopher Columbus, penned those words as he set out to introduce his native continent to yet farther and unimagined shores, to a land that came to be known as the New World, the Americas.

He set sail the day after Tishah B'Av, the national Jewish day of mourning. According to Jewish tradition, Tishah B'Av nurtures the seeds of Jewish redemption, too, and the lands Columbus discovered were, in fact, to become a welcome refuge for countless Jews in a dark and distant future. It would be nearly a century, though, before European colonists began settling North America.

The first large migration to America, following the establishment of various French and Spanish outposts and settlements, took place in 1630, when English Puritans founded the Massachusetts Bay Colony. Similar colonies sprung up in what are today Connecticut and Rhode Island.

The settlers viewed the Native Americans they found in the land with curiosity, fear and a healthy measure of chauvinism. Among the first Europeans to lay eyes on the Narragansetts, one of the major Algonquian tribes, was the Italian explorer Giovanni da Verazzano, who, in the early 1500s, called them "the finest-looking tribe and the handsomest...that we have found in our voyage."

Once the Puritans had settled New England, however, it wasn't long before the Narragansetts and their Wampanoag neighbors found themselves embroiled in a life-and-death struggle with those they perceived — with every justification — as invaders.

The settlers regarded the native tribes, with equal justification, as heathens. (The Narragansetts informed Roger Williams, the famous British-born clergyman, that they worshipped no fewer than thirty-seven "principal gods.") Unfortunately for the Narragansetts, their pagan status inspired the settlers to massacre them with much the same relish their forebears had displayed centuries earlier during the Crusades in the Old World. The savagery of the Puritan attacks on the natives they themselves called "savages" would scarcely be believable had the settlers not punctiliously and triumphantly recorded them. They saw it as their Christian duty to root out the "godless Indians" and went about their work with efficient determination.

By the end of the 1670s, the Narragansett tribe had been decimated from as many as 5,000 people to fewer than 600.

In Jewish mystical thought, the dispersion of the Jewish people after the destruction of the Second Temple was no mere punishment; it was — and is — an opportunity, too, not only to appreciate the specialness of our own land, but to grow from the experience of living among other peoples, to set an example of holiness for the world, and, perhaps most important, to attract non-Jews to Judaism. For while Judaism is not a proselytizing religion, and while it accepts moral gentiles as they are, it does allow converts. According to Jewish tradition, there are "migrant" Jewish souls trapped in far-flung lands, "sparks" long lost and adrift in the farthest reaches of human habitation. Before the era of the Messiah, when humanity will unite in homage to God, those stray sparks will blaze their way to their rightful place and rejoin the Jewish people.

While the explorations of the fifteenth century stretched the horizons of European commerce and knowledge of the world, they also expanded the Jewish people's diaspora, and with it the Jewish purpose. Places where the word "Jew" had never been heard became places of Jewish settlement. And peoples who had lived literally worlds apart came to meet, marry and even provide, in their offspring, novel repositories for migrant Jewish souls.

During the first half of this century, in a small New England town, there lived a family known as the Firmans, descendants of the seventeenth-century Narragansett tribe. Some members of the clan still regarded themselves as Indian to the core, often participating in tribal reunions and powwows. Others were less passionate about their roots, though proud of them nonetheless. Donald Firman was one of the former and his sister Martha, one of the latter.

In 1943, when Martha met and married George Gomes, a man whose family had immigrated to North America several years earlier from Brava, a Cape Verdean island whose population's deep, tangled roots wound back to Africa and Portugal, it was a marriage made in heaven.

CHAPTER 1

Troubled Youth

They worked at the same textile mill, Martha as a spinner, George as a dyer. When a mutual friend introduced them, she was immediately struck by his crazily multicolored shirt — the product of the work he did all day — and by the swarthy, handsome face that smiled above its polychromatic collar. For his part, he was drawn to her shyness. There was something noble about her, something pure and special that he found hard to articulate but equally hard to ignore.

Whenever he passed his new acquaintance at the mill, he smiled and wished her "Good morning" or "Good afternoon." His politeness proved a good investment: when he finally asked her for a date, her shyness didn't keep her from eagerly accepting.

Within a year, they were married.

George's mother came from Iberian stock and was born on the Cape Verdean island of Brava. When her captain husband perished at sea, she married the Portuguese bearer of the sad news. John Gomes brought his new wife to America in 1916, and the following year George was born.

Martha's father was a Mohawk Indian who had embraced Catholicism. Her mother was a full-blooded Narragansett descended from ancestral chiefs, and though she, too, had adopted Christianity and regularly attended a Baptist church, she took pains to maintain her tribal ties. She dutifully took her children, Martha and Donald, to the yearly powwow, at which members of the tribe would gather on their ancestral land and perform or watch ceremonial dances and prayers. Donald was deeply moved by the powwows, though his mother and sister saw them more as family reunions than religious rites.

George Gomes worked two jobs to support his wife and their seven children.

Abel was their fourth child and his parents often noted how different he was from his siblings, how he never needed scolding. Martha took particular pride in her son's politeness and consideration for others; Abel was studious, serious and bright.

His parents' only complaint was that Abel seldom joined in any family fun, such as watching sitcoms together. He never acted with condescension, though, and his family never doubted his love for them. He simply had other things to do, like studying and reading. The closest he got to recreation was indulging his interest and talent in music. He learned to play various wind instruments and practiced religiously, finally settling on the flute. Snatches of soulful melodies would drift into the family room and weave their way through the tangle of prerecorded laughter. But nobody minded; Abel was Abel. What he lacked in shared interests, he more than made up for with his equanimity, industriousness, honesty and clear, logical mind.

Unlike most of his peers, Abel did not smoke. One biology class display of a smoker's lung had been enough to dissuade him. He seemed unwilling to exercise the teenage privilege of ignoring reality. If a path made sense, he'd follow it; if it seemed harmful, illogical or wrong, he simply opted out.

Sunday mornings found the television off and the Gomes family at church. All the children embraced their father's Catholicism, especially Abel and his youngest sister, Wanda, and everyone attended a Catholic school during the week.

In the tenth grade, Abel felt his first cramp of disillusionment with the Catholic faith.

"It is so important to realize," Brother Phillip taught Abel's class, "that only through the true and ancient Church can a sinner achieve forgiveness and salvation. When people profess Christian belief and claim to live Christian lives but reject the true Church, their claim to spiritual salvation is empty. They are being misled by the Devil himself."

Almost imperceptibly, Abel frowned as a thought formed in his mind.

"Does that mean that even good, moral, church-going people who aren't Catholic are damned?" another boy in class asked.

"The Kingdom of God," the Brother answered after a moment's hesitation, "is available to everyone. It is a gift. But a gift must be received. If it is ignored, then one forfeits its benefits."
Abel's thought crystallized in the form of his grandmother, whose own mother had worshipped the multiple deities of the Narragansetts.

On the board, Brother Phillip wrote, *"Extra ecclesiam nulla salus"* — "There is no salvation outside the Church."

Abel's classmate spoke up again:

"But aren't there millions of non-Catholics who live just the kind of life you teach us to live, even though they belong to other churches? Aren't there a lot more of them than there are of us?"
Brother Phillip's kind eyes showed his sorrow at that unfortunate fact, but he managed to smile and the class laughed quietly, a little nervously. Returning to the board, he added a second Latin phrase neatly underneath the first:

"Salvandorum paucitas, damnadorum multitudo."

"Few are the saved..." the Brother began to translate, but Abel's mind raced ahead. By the time Brother Phillip had finished speaking, Abel's thoughts were elsewhere.

Once the first crack appeared in the dam of Abel's Catholicism, others quickly developed. He listened closely when his teachers related how Jesus' followers had become the "new chosen," how the "new law" had superseded the old, and an odd discomfort set in.

"Christianity offered Jews freedom from the fetters of the ancient Law," one teacher explained, "but their leaders had become too obsessed with dietary laws, ritual purity and the like to hear the message of love and concern for one's fellow, or even to recognize the arrival of their own messiah."

Why had the Old Testament laws needed abolishment, Abel found himself thinking, just to promote goodwill among men? And wasn't concern for others no less a part of the Old Testament?

"The Jews of the time were more concerned," the teacher continued, "with what *entered* their mouths than with what *emerged* from them!"

Couldn't they have incorporated both? Abel countered to himself. *Couldn't they have fulfilled the laws God had given them along with His new will? And just what did "God's new will" mean, anyway? Why had the Old Testament been given at all if it had only been temporary?*

Abel recalled how he had once toyed with joining the priesthood. No more, though. The abundant inconsistencies in his faith, the myriad "mysteries" it laid down like roadblocks before reasonable inquiry, and the uncomfortable implications of its tenets had rendered that dream antithetical to his commitment to honesty. While he did not abandon Catholicism yet, he began to feel that it was smothering something in his soul.

Had that something been just a garden-variety quest for identity, it would have had ample opportunity to express itself in Abel's Indian heritage. His uncle Donald had taken that path and immersed himself in their common Narragansett ancestry. He considered the Narragansett customs and beliefs his own, no less than the land on which he lived, the United States government notwithstanding. He attended the tribe's powwows and danced its sacred dances, carrying on a centuries-old tradition. On occasion, Abel would accompany his uncle to a powwow, but he always sat bashfully to the side, often impressed with the pageantry but never with its relevance.

By the time he graduated from high school, Abel considered his religious heritage an increasingly unwieldy burden. Still, old habits die hard and he continued to attend church regularly. When the time came, he even chose a Catholic college.

Even as a business administration major at Loyola College, Abel was required to take several religion courses. One of his teachers, a priest, shared his surprise at his students' ignorance of the Old Testament and Judaism in general.

"The Jewish heritage belongs to Jews and Christians alike," he informed his entirely Catholic class, "and none of us can claim to understand Christianity without a firm knowledge of our roots, which are largely Jewish."

The priest chided the class about how the Jewish students he had taught, though seldom religious, seemed much more knowledgeable about the Old Testament than their Christian classmates, even though the Old Testament is an integral part of the Christian bible.

Something in Abel was piqued by the priest's mild reprimand. He really hadn't thought much about modern Jews or Judaism — and certainly not in any relationship to his own religion. He had known, of course, that Christianity had begun as an offshoot of Judaism, that Jesus had been a Jew whose coreligionists had rejected him as their savior. But now he had to consider the existence of Jews *qua* Jews two millennia after Jesus. Years later, he would recall the irony of first confronting Judaism as a modern reality — and a positive one, no less — by way of a priest. At the time, though, it was less revelation than curiosity, an interesting fact to ponder: Jews existed and studied their Bible even today. It put an intriguing spin on his dormant knowledge that the Jewish religion had preceded and even spawned his own.

Abel's only other Jewish "connection" during his early college years was his linguistics teacher, Ms. Rosengarden. Though he would eventually graduate cum laude, Abel felt she consistently graded him unfairly.

CHAPTER 2

Salvaged Dreams

Returning from their honeymoon, the newlyweds found their small Polish town in radical, terrible flux. It was 1939.

Mere days after invading the country, Nazi troops had entered the village. Rivka was frantic, and the strange calm among so many of the villagers only frightened her more. They seemed to consider the German presence just some temporary inconvenience, a minor blemish on the face of Poland that would clear up soon enough.

One colorless fall day shortly after the invasion, Rivka was suddenly seized by an uncontrollable spasm of logic. The realization that the Jews of the village should run for their lives streaked across her consciousness like a blazing comet.

As if pursued by a demon, Rivka ran to her sister's home, just a few houses down the narrow, dirt road. Bursting through the front door, she found her sister and family engaged in a card game. The players all looked up in unison at their panicked visitor.

"What is it, Rivkele? What happened?"

"We've all got to leave!" the young bride exclaimed, out of breath. "There is no hope for us here with the Germans in charge! We must run!"

The others only smiled at her agitation.

"Rivka," one of them began calmly, slowly, "you mustn't jump to conclusions or do anything rash. Sometimes it's best to see where things are going before making irreversible decisions."

"Think of all you'd be giving up if you left," another player interjected. "You don't even know if you'll end up anywhere better, and in the meanwhile you will have lost everything you have. Think of the wedding gifts, the furniture you bought, the lovely dishes…"

Rivka couldn't believe her ears. *What was wrong with them?!* she screamed in her thoughts.

"What are a few pieces of wood and glass worth if we're all dead?!" she shouted.

The card players looked at each other, some smiling nervously, some sighing softly in tender condescension.

Rivka just clenched her fists in frustration and ran out the door.

Only days later, the Nazis began rounding up the town's men folk. Struggling to be calm, to see things as optimistically as the others, Rivka reluctantly let her husband go, but she immediately vowed never to give him up again if he ever returned. As it happened, her Yossel was released just two days afterward, his detention merely a temporary measure.

When the Germans announced a second roundup a week later, Rivka remembered her promise and refused to relinquish her husband. Convincing him to don his mother's clothing, she told the Germans who came to get him that he had left, and that they could search the house if they wanted. The ruse worked.

Though their friends and relatives insisted that the oppression would soon pass, Yossel and Rivka saw no hope. Expecting the worst — and their first child — they set off immediately for Russia, leaving dishes, furniture and family behind forever.

Despite his devoutly Chassidic upbringing, Yossel had long since rejected his forebears' antiquated faith and proudly identified himself as a socialist and secular Zionist. Still and all, he and his wife had, if a diminished faith in Judaism, an unwavering one in the Jewish people. Refusing Russian citizenship, the couple spent the next five years in a Soviet labor camp, determined to survive the war one way or another. Their resolve was sorely tested, however — by hunger, pain, the loss of their newborn son to typhus, and Rivka's own extended and nearly fatal illness.

By the war's end, Rivka had recovered and was carrying their second child. They boarded a train leaving Russia but were forced off when Rivka went into labor early in the journey. Just as the frightened couple thought they had lost their chance to escape their refuge-turned-prison, a second train appeared out of nowhere and the family boarded it: mother, father and new daughter, Ariella.

Soon enough, they would leave the continent, glue together what pieces of their lives they had salvaged, and raise their daughter in a new promised land called America. Even their inflated memories of Lodz and Cracow were completely overwhelmed by the magnificence of their new home, Los Angeles. They dreamt that their daughter would grow up without fear or want, free of the burdens of totalitarianism and religion.

CHAPTER 3

Impressive Connections

With his sterling undergraduate record, Abel had no trouble gaining entrance to a prestigious Colorado graduate school that was widely recognized in the field of international business, his career of choice. His first semester at the Institute for International Economics, at the end of 1973, went well and he began to plan his second.

One early fall day, standing in line to register for a class, he felt a sudden compulsion to turn around. Surrendering to the urge, he found himself looking straight into the powerfully expressive eyes of a young woman standing several students behind him. As it happened, she had been staring at his jet-black hair, which he wore long during his college days. Surprised by his unexpected turn toward her, she looked away.

Several days later, in his marketing class, Abel overheard a man ask a woman for her phone number. Glancing toward them, he was surprised to see the same eyes, their warmth and intelligence unmistakable.

Motivated by some obscure part of himself, Abel then did something entirely out of character. Turning to the woman, he asked her with a smile, "Me, too?" He was rather amazed at his own words, and all the more so when the lady obliged.

He dialed her number that very night and they spoke briefly. Her name was Ariella Lipkin and she was recently divorced. Though she was several years older than Abel, the pair became increasingly friendly over the next few months.

It was a simple friendship, nothing serious. At the time, Ariella was dating someone closer to her own age; Abel was just someone she enjoyed talking with.

Their discussions were usually light and airy, unmemorable but fun. Sometimes, though, they would touch on precarious conversational ground. If there had been a sign posted, it would have read: "Beware of Argument." The topic was usually men and women.

Ariella was an ardent, sometimes strident feminist, and her commitment to the women's movement occasionally but noisily clashed with Abel's old-fashioned, homey ideas about male and female roles. But even their disagreements, like those about the value of intellectualism (which Abel defined as "snobbery"), were left behind once their positions had been staked out. Some subtle but overpowering element in their camaraderie seemed to erase all the lines they drew in the conceptual sand, overshadowing the fact that — as Abel once put it — "we're really incompatible."

As the school year drew to a close, however, the two friends drifted out of touch.

That summer, as Ariella was on her way to visit a friend in another city, her vacation plans were rudely interrupted. Cruising along a winding mountain road, she nudged the steering wheel just enough to negotiate a curve, but her car suddenly seemed to be taking other orders. Through the windshield, she saw clear, blue sky instead of the double yellow line, and realized that she and the car were, for a long, crazy moment, airborne. There was too little time to panic before a loud, abrupt crunch announced the end of her flight. Most of the sound, it turned out, was the metal of the car; some of it, though, was her tibia. She spent the rest of her summer in a hospital, wondering at her simultaneous misfortune and good luck. Only years later would she see the unmistakable hand of Providence in her accident and recognize the subtle, intricate patterns that formed in its wake.

When she finally arrived at school for the new semester, she was two weeks late and in a wheelchair, with a large, immobilizing cast on her leg. Several days after her return, as a girlfriend wheeled her along the path to her off-campus apartment, Ariella sensed a figure growing larger in her periphery. It suddenly materialized into Abel, who, as it happened, lived in the same garden apartment complex. His deep concern for Ariella's condition showed in his face, and when she related what had happened, she received the sympathy and commiseration she'd expected. Something more, though, was forthcoming.

That evening, as Ariella lay on the couch feeling, as usual of late, a little sorry for herself and a little angry at no one in particular, there was a knock on the door.

"It's open," she called out, presuming that burglars didn't knock.

Abel's head poked out from behind the partially opened door.

"May I come in?" he asked sheepishly.

"Sure."

He did, carrying a bag of groceries, and proceeded to cook Ariella dinner.

The next morning, Abel arrived early to take Ariella to class, and then to take her home again and prepare her dinner. He took her garbage out and did her laundry, and she found herself not only overwhelmed at his goodwill but enjoying his company more than ever. She let her boyfriend lapse.

Raised by adamantly socialist, universalist parents, Ariella took little notice of Abel's complexion, and less still of his religion.

By 1974's winter break, Ariella's leg had healed and she and Abel set off to visit various friends and relatives around the country. Eventually, they found themselves in central Massachusetts, in Abel's parents' living room. The Gomeses found Ariella pleasant and understood her to be just what she had been introduced as, a college friend of their son's. Abel had said nothing about any future plans for there weren't any.

From Abel's parents' house, he and Ariella boarded their umpteenth bus, this one headed for Tennessee, where friends of hers lived. The trip was uneventful and the stay no less so — at least for the first few days.

One night, though, the two attended a college basketball game. During a lull in the action, Abel suddenly turned to Ariella and asked her to marry him.

Earlier that day, they had spoken of marriage as a concept, spurred by the fact that the friends they were visiting had recently been married. Abel had remarked how important it was to plan so crucial a decision in life slowly and carefully, for a haphazard, spontaneous approach could lead to disaster. Ariella, the memory of her own careful, deceased marriage still all too vivid, had insisted that fate often wreaked havoc with human orchestrations. Abel had weighed her words silently for a few moments and then coolly changed the subject.

And now, only several hours later, Ariella sat staring at Abel, his words dancing crazily in her lap.

She was certainly surprised by his proposal but the sheer irony of it enchanted her. Abel himself was somewhat startled by what he'd said — just as he had been the first time he had seen Ariella and asked for her phone number.

"Could I think for a minute?" she asked.

"Of course," he mumbled in reply.

The game resumed but the pensive pair didn't notice.

After what seemed like a long time, Ariella looked up and said yes. The crowd cheered a successful long shot.

Shortly thereafter, to the puzzlement but sincere congratulations of both sets of parents, the pair announced their engagement. True to their social and political convictions, Ariella's folks considered neither Abel's ethnic background nor his religion. Abel's mother and father were equally accepting of Ariella; her Jewish roots were a curiosity but nothing more. The couple tied the knot in a small, simple ceremony before a justice of the peace.

After their graduation, Abel and Ariella looked for work. Calm and unassuming, Abel found the emerging and disturbing pattern of his job-hunting experiences difficult to ignore.

Scheduled for an interview with a seemingly eager employer, he'd show up well-dressed and on time. But immediately on meeting the interviewer, he'd sense that something had gone awry, even before either of them had spoken a word. Once, he had actually been offered a job over the phone, only to arrive at the company and find that the position had, uh, been filled in the meantime.

Abel began to realize that although his skin was lighter than some slightly overbaked card-carrying Caucasians he knew, to at least part of the white world, he was still apparently not white enough.

Abel's family was as multicolored as their Cape Verdean heritage. His grandparents and parents were as lily-white as Ariella's Polish forebears, yet uncles, aunts and siblings were dark enough to be classified as Hispanic or even black by some whites unaccustomed to the finer shades of ethnic diversity. There were dark-skinned relatives in Abel's mother's family, too, the Native American part of his lineage.

Abel had never considered skin color anything more than one of those variables of life, like eye color or the ability to roll one's tongue or raise a single eyebrow. As a result, he had always regarded racism, at least in the modern, white-collar world, as something of an anachronism. Now, though, he couldn't help but recall a painful incident from his college years.

Abel had hoped to spend his junior year in Spain, studying on an academic merit scholarship. When his application was rejected, he met with the dean of the program to find out why. The dean spoke up a storm but said nothing, dissembling with all the skill unique to academics and politicians. Abel couldn't fathom why he was being denied the honorarium he had earned, but he accepted what seemed impossible to change. Only much later did he hear of a pattern of overt racism within Loyola.

Now, as a job-hunter finding irrational roadblocks wherever he turned, the memory of his lost European year percolated in his thoughts. America was in a recession, he told himself. But in his heart, Abel knew that the economic climate had much less to do with his disappointments than the racial one.

Fortunately for the couple's financial future, if not for Abel's self-image, Ariella landed work soon enough — in Manhattan. Abel still had no offers, so in the summer of 1975 he and his wife moved to New York.

Though their apartment was a stone's throw from the large and well-known Lincoln Square Synagogue, Ariella never went to services. On occasion, Abel would ask her something about Judaism but she would simply answer, "I don't know, dear."

Ariella's parents had sometimes talked about the Holocaust but they attributed the horrors of the war years to an imperfect world. In their view, socialism was the Jew's hope, not Judaism. Ariella's familiarity with her religious heritage was limited to memories of High Holiday services — which were geared more toward cantorial performance than spiritual benefit — and her family's Passover seder. The latter was a simple affair: her father would place any bread out of sight, take out some matzo, read a few selections from a Haggadah, and that was it. As a girl, she had attended Hebrew school briefly — until she persuaded her parents that she hated it. In truth, she didn't; she simply saw no point in sitting through instruction that had even less to do with her life than the arithmetic and social studies she had to put up with at school.

"How can you say you know nothing about Judaism when you're so proud of being Jewish?" Abel would ask his wife.

"Abel, I'm a Jew by nationality, not religion. The Jewish people is my people but I simply don't know anything about Judaism. My heart's Jewish, not my kitchen."

To Abel, Ariella's words rang hollow. He wanted to know more about his wife's identity. Though she considered her Jewishness merely peripheral, he couldn't shake the feeling that she was somehow blinding herself. He even suspected that some element of her Jewishness had attracted him in the first place.

Meanwhile, their discussions on the subject remained purely theoretical. Like most Manhattanite professionals, they were too busy just trying to make it to complicate their lives with any hands-on, old-time religion.

One afternoon, however, an innocent stroll home from a job interview took Abel past the famed Spanish-Portuguese synagogue on Central Park West, one of the oldest Jewish congregations in the country. He stopped dead in his tracks and stared at the imposing, columned edifice and the three arches that marked its entrance. He was intrigued by more than just the noteworthy architecture — and he knew why.

His Portuguese studies in college had emphasized not only language but history. Consequently, Abel knew that several unusually fertile centuries of Portuguese history were bound up with an important era of Jewish history. He recalled how his language professor at Loyola had spoken often about Portuguese Jewish history. He knew that the Jews of the late Middle Ages had fared even better in Portugal than in Spain, the excesses of the clergy in the latter land largely prevented — or at least postponed — by Portuguese leaders. He also knew that Portugal had ultimately expelled her Jews, too, in 1496, forcibly baptizing thousands of Jewish children before their parents could leave the country. And he knew about the fate of many Portuguese Marranos, or secret Jews, when Pope Clement VII introduced the Inquisition into the land.

But the earlier, illustrious centuries of Jewish development and growth in Spain and Portugal were what stood out in Abel's memory. And here before him stood one of the most celebrated repositories of that era, a cache of the artwork, literature, culture and learning of the Spanish-Portuguese Jewish world.

He didn't go in. It seemed too sacred a place to enter without his wife. After all, he reasoned, Ariella was the Jewish one; her presence in the synagogue would be a legitimate indulgence of her heritage rather than a questionable one of his curiosity.

When Abel arrived home, he shared his desire to visit the synagogue with his wife, but his excitement proved less than contagious. Ariella didn't see what the big deal was. Sensing how much it meant to her husband, however, she consented to accompany him.

"Now this is rich," she said as they approached their destination. "Here I am a Jew, and you're the one who wants to go to synagogue."

Abel smiled.

"It might be a synagogue," he reminded her, "but it's a piece of Portuguese history, too."

Ariella knew full well that her husband spoke fluent Portuguese and that his paternal roots stretched back to the west coast of the Iberian peninsula.

"True, but you don't exactly make a point of visiting every museum exhibit with a Portuguese connection."

She had a point, Abel knew, but he didn't give it too much thought.

The synagogue was itself something of a museum, with a rabbi instead of a curator. Rabbi Veniste, himself of Portuguese extraction, met them as they entered.

"We hope we're not intruding," Abel began, "but we were wondering if we might look around the synagogue for a while."

"No intrusion at all," the rabbi answered them through a polite smile nestled in a curly beard. "The synagogue is open to the public."

Rabbi Veniste showed the couple some artifacts whose creators' bones lay far across the Atlantic: silver Torah crowns and pointers, goblets, furniture and the like, as well as Torah scrolls, rams' horns, and Hebrew prayer books with Spanish or Portuguese translation. After explaining elements of the building's architecture and describing the Sephardic tradition of prayer, the rabbi politely but pointedly asked Abel if he was Jewish. Abel shyly answered in the negative but hastily presented Ariella's credentials as his excuse for sitting in a synagogue excitedly studying a Jewish prayer book.

As Abel sat engrossed in the books and their surroundings, Ariella reflected on how strangely foreign a synagogue felt to her own soul. The high, austere walls seemed to hem in and stifle whatever Jewish feelings she could summon. She thought of the holiday services her parents had taken her to and how she had known, even as a child, that they had intended the experience as spectacle, not spiritual; her father's faith was socialism and he had always felt more at home with a *Forward* — the Yiddish-language "worker's paper" — than a prayer book. Still, she thought, there was an odd ambience here, a certain comfort amid the severity. Sensibly, she wrote it off to her husband's happiness at being there.

"Maybe you've got Marrano blood in you, Abel," Ariella quipped as they left the synagogue.

"You never know," Abel replied quietly.

Several days later, Abel asked Ariella if she might be interested in attending services at the Spanish-Portuguese synagogue on the High Holidays, only weeks away.

"What?"

"I just thought you might like to go."

"Why?"

"I'm not sure," Abel admitted, "but I'd only feel comfortable myself if you were going, too."

Ariella couldn't believe her husband's sudden fixation. She tried not to let her incredulity show, but made no such effort to hide her own feelings about any such formal religious expression.

"I don't think so, Abel. I really wish I shared this desire of yours to experience the service, but I just know how uncomfortable I'd feel if I went."

She waited for a reaction that wasn't forthcoming and then tried another tack.

"Abel, even if I went with you, we'd be sitting miles apart from each other. It's an Orthodox synagogue. The women sit up in the balcony."

Abel was taken aback.

"And did you know," Ariella continued, well on the offensive now, "that we'd have to buy *tickets* to be admitted?"

"Tickets?" Abel asked in confusion.

Ha, Ariella thought. I've scored a hit.

"Yup," she said matter-of-factly. "Can't get in without them."

"Come on. You're not serious."

"I am," she insisted. "Believe me, Abel, I wouldn't lie about something like this."

Now that is bizarre, Abel thought. But what had already dissuaded him from going was the fact that even if Ariella managed to drag herself along with him, she clearly wouldn't share his enthusiasm for being there. And he knew he wouldn't feel right experiencing something so personal when she was entirely disinterested. She was, after all, his wife, part of him, not to mention his only real connection with a Jewish service to begin with.

So they didn't go. And Judaism remained on the outskirts of their existence, even in the heart of the city with more Jews than any other.

CHAPTER 4

Unexpected Blessings

The young couple didn't stay in New York for long. Within a few months, Abel was offered a marketing position with a manufacturing concern, and he had no intention of letting the opportunity slip away. He had interviewed for the job so these people knew just what he looked like, and they still wanted him. He wanted them, too.

The Gomeses would have to move, as it happened, to the small but growing New England town where Abel had been born and raised and where his parents still lived. When he first learned about the position available in his hometown, a strange feeling in the pit of his stomach brought a wry smile to his face. Forces larger than he seemed to be taking him back to his roots. He didn't suspect that deeper roots yet were beckoning in the distance.

New York had been an interesting place to live but it had never really been home, so neither Abel nor Ariella found it hard to say goodbye. Besides, Ariella felt confident that she would land work in their new place of residence. So the two of them followed Interstate 95 north to their future.

Hope Heights, Massachusetts, is just small enough to be quaint yet large enough to matter. The high-tech industry that had spread through the region like Boston ivy had made Hope Heights the community of choice for many of the area's new residents. Their influx had transformed the sleepy town into a small metropolis of sorts. One could still meet one's barber, banker or doctor on a typical stroll downtown, but the number of strangers one saw between familiar faces had grown considerably throughout the '70s. Buildings whose size and design were once expected only of New York or Boston had sprung up in the business district, and suits and ties began to rival flannel shirts and work boots as the local costume.

For their first month in Hope Heights, the couple stayed with Abel's parents. Ariella found work as the administrator of a state Department of Education grant program, and both she and her husband focused on their jobs. Life seemed to be going as planned, but its direction was soon to shift decisively and unexpectedly.

Like urban professionals before them, Abel and Ariella had planned their family no less carefully than their investment portfolio. Before complicating their lives with kids, they both wanted to find themselves and to become secure in their relationship and in their respective careers. So the sudden suspicion, quickly confirmed, that Ariella was pregnant came as a great surprise.

At first, Ariella felt that it was unfair. It was as if something from without were fooling with her life. The laws of physiology, causality and reason had betrayed her and invited the ghost of chance into her world. Her discomfort, however, soon enough gave way to the sublime feelings of impending motherhood.

The couple moved into an apartment just below that of Abel's brother and tried to settle into their work. They wanted to minimize the disruption their imminent responsibility would surely bring, though they could hardly ignore the approaching roads they had no maps for.

On one visit to the obstetrician, Abel voiced a concern that had begun to occupy his mind uncomfortably often.

"If it's a boy, do you know anyone qualified to perform the circumcision?"

As a veteran obstetrician who prided himself on keeping abreast of the latest medical trends, the Jewish doctor eyed Abel curiously.

"Are you sure you want to opt for circumcision altogether, Mr. Gomes? There is something of an emerging consensus against it these days."

Abel nodded decisively, affirmatively.

"Well, let me ask you, what exactly do you mean by `qualified'?"

Abel was only slightly taken aback.

"You see, my wife is Jewish, Doctor, and we'll need the circumcision done the way the Jewish religion requires. Are there any ritual circumcisers in the area?"

The doctor glanced hopefully at Ariella but found no alliance in her eyes. He then turned back to the dark and unmistakably serious man who had addressed him.

"Well, I myself am fully qualified to perform circumcisions and have indeed done many in my day for Jewish parents."

The couple smiled, secure in the knowledge that, though the pregnancy had taken them by surprise, at least circumcision had been properly arranged.

Several weeks and one sonogram later, they learned that they were expecting twins — and that they needn't have considered circumcision.

Naming two baby girls at one shot was a tall order, and Ariella readily ceded the honor to Abel. He settled first on Daphna, the name of a teacher he had once had. He had always liked the name, if not the teacher. Inexplicably inspired by the enchanting name of a jazz singer he had once heard, he called his second child Ruth.

When the new parents arrived home with the babies, Abel's family was there to greet them. The infants were cuddled and passed around and Ariella was dutifully fussed over.

"When will the `time' be?" asked the elder Mr. Gomes during a lull in the festive conversation. Ariella's face registered puzzlement but Abel knew what his father was referring to. He decided to translate for his wife and let her respond.

"A christening," he said simply.
Ariella's puzzlement quickly yielded to something stronger, sharper, more focused, a feeling she immediately verbalized.

"The babies won't be having a christening," she pronounced. "They're Jewish."

Abel's parents had always been dedicated Christians, but they had never used their faith as a pedestal from which to disparage others. Abel took their tolerance for granted and knew they would not be angry with Ariella. Still, they wondered whether her assertiveness might have less to do with religious commitment than with some post-partum hormonal flux. Abel's father tried to up the emotional ante.

"Ariella, at the `time,' baby gifts are given by all the relatives and friends!"

Ariella smiled but it was not a concessionary smile.

Abel's mother continued the feeble assault.

"And, dear, you'll get everything you need for the babies without having to go to a hundred stores. Not to mention things for yourself."

Abel watched as his wife turned her smile down several degrees to the vicinity of absolute zero. He conjured up a medieval image of a Portuguese bishop and nun trying to coax a stubborn Jew into the baptismal font with assurances of material wealth and acceptance into the Christian community. Then Abel caught himself and erased the image, embarrassed at having so cast his parents, who were only trying to maintain a warm family tradition. Still, he silently egged Ariella on in her frosty response to his parents' pleas. Then he realized that his responsibility went beyond moral support.

"Mom, Dad," he interrupted, "the twins are Jewish because their mother is Jewish — that's the way it works in Judaism — so it really wouldn't be right to christen them."

"Look," conceded Abel's father, "you're the parents, do what you want. I just think you're giving up a great opportunity to provide all sorts of things for your kids."

"For goodness sake," Ariella interjected, at a considerably higher pitch than she had intended, "gifts aren't the goal of life!" Then, surprised at her own agitation, she added, "But if it's that important to you, then go ahead and have your ceremony. But I won't be attending."

"Oh, don't be silly, Ariella," Abel's mother announced conclusively. "We wouldn't think of having a `time' without you there. If you feel so strongly about your religion, then we accept that."

"Anyway," Dad added with an exaggeratedly sly smile, "there's always the kitchen sink when you're not looking."

Ariella found it within her to smile at that image of surreptitious baptism. She was relieved at her victory though still somewhat baffled by her own fervor. *If you feel so strongly about your religion....* Her mother-in-law's words bounced about in her mind.

Later that night, after her in-laws had left, Ariella played with her puzzlement. She knew she had no commitment to Jewish practice. For heaven's sake, she reminded herself, she had married a non-Jew! And yet, every so often something made her feel Jewish, even furiously so at times — as she had that afternoon. It was probably because her parents' Jewishness had mattered in such a terrible way, she ruminated. In a sense, she was herself a Holocaust survivor. As such, she mused, the seeds of her determination that her own children's Jewishness remain unsullied may have germinated in the dark dangers her family had faced long ago.

In fact, the still, small Jew within her had spoken up at odder times, such as when Abel had bought some meat she hadn't recognized. Somewhat astounded by her ignorance, he'd identified it as pork chops.

"Oh," she'd reacted coolly, "I don't think I've ever had any before. How should I prepare them?" Abel had suggested that she bread and fry them. As it happened, the only breading in her pantry had been matzo meal.

As the chops sizzled, the Jew deep in her gut had sneered at the sight and smell of the pig pieces bonding with the powdery crumbs of the Jewish "bread of affliction." Then, while she'd stood over the frying pan, the phone had rung. It had been her mother on the line, long-distance.

"Did I catch you in the middle of making supper?" Mama had asked.

To Ariella, the little Jew inside her now openly snickering, her mother's question had sounded like an accusation.

"Sort of," she replied hesitantly.

"Oh, then I'll call back later. What're you making, dear?"

Why was she asking that?

Ariella had hesitated for an uncomfortable instant, then blurted out, Veal chops!" before hastily composing herself and shyly signing off.

Ariella smiled at the memory and wondered at its awkwardness. True, her parents had never brought pork into their home when she had been growing up, but neither had they made any effort to keep kosher. Their dietary habits had been just that, habits — Eastern European in origin and devoid of any sacred imperatives. Yet the pork chops' sizzle had awakened the tiny Jew within her and given him a good, cynical chuckle.

Ariella's thoughts drifted as she prepared for a much-needed night's sleep that she knew the apartment's new occupants would allow her only in installments. She thought about the little girls she had been entrusted with, how they wouldn't remain infants for long, how it wasn't too soon to begin planning for their education, and how they would really need some sort of Jewish environment.

CHAPTER 5

Crucial Encounters

Fluorescent light reflected from the rabbi's bald, uncovered pate. He folded his hands, leaned forward across his desk and smiled quizzically at his visitor.

"I'm afraid I don't quite understand what the problem is, Mr. Gomes. I think you and your wife have made a wise choice by enrolling your daughters in the Jewish Community Center's preschool program. Deciding to raise your children as Jews is exemplary and I commend you for it."

"There really wasn't any decision involved," Abel explained. "Ariella is Jewish, and the way we understand it, that means our children are, too."

The rabbi nodded sagely in agreement.

"Indeed they are. And furthermore, with your fine attitude, you have taken an important step toward creating a strong, lasting marriage. We in the Reform movement deal daily with marriages that are disintegrating because of conflicts caused by spouses' different faiths and divergent plans for their children."

Having spoken his piece, the rabbi paused and then remembered where he had been heading. "So again, I have to say that whatever is troubling you eludes me."

Abel hadn't realized how explicit he needed to be.

"Well," he began cautiously, "since my family is Jewish and I want them to feel fully Jewish, I would like to do everything I can to help them."

"Ye-es?" the rabbi intoned slowly, the way he liked to conclude a responsive reading.

This is ridiculous, Abel chided himself. He had discussed the idea with Ariella countless times since enrolling the girls in preschool. Why was he having such a devilish time getting the words out?

"Uh, what I'm wondering about is the possibility of converting," he heard someone say, and a moment later he realized that the words had apparently grown impatient and marched out on their own.

The rabbi looked no less puzzled for Abel's confession.

"Why, that's a wonderful idea, Mr. Gomes, but why didn't you just say so? Conversion is an excellent option for someone in your position. I hadn't brought it up myself simply because I didn't want to pressure you in any way. But what are your concerns about the idea?"

"Well, Rabbi," Abel explained, relieved at least of the burden of that critical first step, "I'm naturally concerned about the requirements for conversion. This is a big decision for me and I guess I'm just plain nervous about it."

"There's no reason for nervousness, Mr. Gomes. By converting to Judaism, you will be joining the ranks of thousands of `Jews by choice' over the centuries, including many illustrious personalities stretching as far back as the Talmudic era."

He then recited the list he had memorized from the excellent chapter on conversion in the rabbinical manual he had received in seminary.

"Furthermore, more than 40% of our members here at River Road Free Temple were not born Jewish; most of them married Jews, as you did. They then opted for conversion, just as you're considering. So you can certainly feel that a support system exists for you."

Abel was less concerned about what company conversion would place him in than about the requirements of the process itself — and the responsibilities of Jewish life.

"Well, what exactly is the conversion procedure?" he ventured.

"As it happens, Mr. Gomes, the procedure is not difficult. It essentially consists of completing a list of readings, some of which you may find somewhat challenging but, I assure you, well worth the effort. Then, you'll be expected to affiliate Jewishly, joining the temple, the Jewish Federation and any other Jewish organizations you choose. Those affiliations will confirm your inclusion in the Jewish community."

The rabbi paused as a hint of discomfort crossed his face. The next part wasn't in the manual but this convert deserved to hear everything.

"But I do feel, uh, I should point out that some will always see a convert as something, well, less than a full Jew...though they are, of course, not acting from a truly Jewish perspective."

Abel listened to the rabbi's words and tried to grasp them.

"You mean the ultra-Orthodox, who don't recognize other types of Jews?"

"Well, the Orthodox are most certainly rejective of the Reform movement. They consider us all sinners, embodiments of evil. But they are of little concern to us and should be of little concern to you. I was referring, uh, to people within the context of the life you'll be leading as a convert to Reform Judaism."

Abel was deeply perplexed and made no effort to hide it.

"Unfortunately, Mr. Gomes, every community, even a liberal, Jewish one, includes people who are at heart chauvinistic, small-minded and prejudiced against those different from themselves. I don't think it will be a major problem for you, but extensive experience has taught me that not all the smiles shown converts are sincere, even in our congregation."

The rabbi decided he had beaten around the bush long enough.

"And being a man of color," he went on, "you may experience even more of that unfortunate attitude than usual..."

Across town, in a very different capacity, Ariella was talking to a rabbi, too.

Having recently landed a job with an engineering firm, Ariella was to offer free energy audits to schools and office buildings as a means of promoting the company's heating and air-conditioning systems. She had just given her pitch to one Rabbi Mordechai Solomon.

"Well," said Rabbi Solomon, his portly frame topped by a bright-red-bearded face and his face by a large skullcap, "Hope Heights Hebrew Day School already has a satisfactory heating system and couldn't afford a new one right now anyway, but if you still want to do the audit and suggest ways that we could conserve energy, that's just fine. But please understand that we're really not in the market for a new system."

"That makes no difference at all, Rabbi Solomon," she said reassuringly, following the script. "The audit puts you under no obligation to us at all. Energy Systems Conversions Inc. is happy to perform the service in the hope that, should you ever need a heating system in the future, you'll remember us."

Ariella felt funny playing the little game that was her job with this endearing, friendly man. She had liked him as soon as he'd welcomed her into his small, book-lined, disheveled office. Throughout her pitch, the rabbi had listened politely, without even a hint of the impatience she had come to expect from her marks. His insightful questions and comments showed that he was not only attentive but fairly sharp to boot.

Ariella took down the required information, confirmed a date for the audit and asked a few polite questions about the school whose principal sat before her. Rabbi Solomon described it as an Orthodox Jewish day school but quickly added that it served the entire Jewish community, for "Orthodox" characterized its educational orientation and Jewish studies faculty, not necessarily its student body. He made several quips as they spoke and Ariella found the idea of an Orthodox rabbi with a sense of humor somewhat incongruous. But there was no denying that his warmth was genuine.

Though Ariella didn't mention it to Rabbi Solomon, Ariella had been well aware of Hope Heights Hebrew Day School even before seeing its name on her assignment sheet. She and Abel had actually discussed it as a possible school for the twins. She had been inclined to dismiss it because of its Orthodox affiliation; the contradictions between her own lifestyle and a system of religion that required withdrawal from reality, different dress and different priorities from those of enlightened society were just too daunting even to think about. Abel had asked her to at least investigate the school, to see what in fact was taught there, but she'd somehow never gotten around to it.

Yet now, ironically, here she was, talking to the school's principal about the place — and enjoying the conversation. Ariella began to have second thoughts about the idea of an Orthodox school for her children. Still, by the time she took leave of the rabbi, she hadn't even mentioned that she was Jewish.

Out in the hall, she saw a modishly dressed young woman with several books under her arm. The woman smiled at her, and Ariella immediately sought to connect with this decidedly non-rabbinical figure.

"Hello," she said, slipping nimbly out of the role she had been playing all morning, "my name is Ariella Lipkin-Gomes, and I was wondering if this school might suit my children's needs." She surprised herself with her smooth transition from commercial fishhook to flesh-and-blood parent. "Oh, it's a very special school," the teacher answered with a pronounced Israeli accent, "and I recommend it highly." Then, realizing she hadn't introduced herself, she added, "Oh, pardon! My name is Tamar Reuveini and I am teaching Hebrew here."

Ariella took her outstretched hand, along with the opportunity to find out more about the school. After all, she had promised Abel she would.

"I'm a little concerned about the fact that it's Orthodox. I mean, I wouldn't want my kids to come home with any crazy ideas or to look down at me for what I am."

"You are Jewish?"

"Yes, but my husband is not."

In a characteristically Israeli way, Tamar waved the matter a<%0>way with a decisive stroke of her hand.

"That's no problem. You would not be the only parents like that here. The school is welcoming all Jewish children and is trying its best to make their parents comfortable."

"But still, isn't it an Orthodox school?"

"Not all Orthodox are like you think. Sure, the rabbis here are wishing everybody was like them but they still know what the real world is like."

Ariella felt a momentary warmth at the words and then wondered at it. After all, she hadn't entered the building with any desire to hear if her children would be accepted there. She knew that she was Jewish and her daughters were, too. She didn't need any Orthodox rabbis to confirm the fact. Still, the warmth washed over her and it felt good.

"Why, thank you so very much," she told Tamar, shaking her hand again.

Tamar waved and disappeared up some stairs, leaving Ariella to her thoughts.

As she walked the few steps to the door, she felt an urge to take a last look down the hall of the school whose sharp edges had just been softened.

What she saw made her heart sink.

Two dark-suited figures were conversing animatedly at the far end of the hall. Each sported a prominent beard and a black hat. Though she couldn't see them very clearly and didn't address them, the fragile crystal of her fantasy had been crushed. She had glimpsed enough in that instant to know that, with all due respect to her new Israeli friend, this was no place for her children — not in a million years.

That night at dinner, Ariella didn't recount her conversation with Tamar but she did allow her imagination to considerably lengthen the two men's beards and fur their hats. Abel listened sympathetically and then shared his own disappointment over his meeting.

"It just felt so empty," he explained to his wife, "like something important was missing. I mean, read some books? That can't be all a conversion to Judaism entails!"

"Abel, what difference does it make? You'll be considered Jewish in the eyes of the temple."

"I don't want to be considered Jewish. I want to be Jewish."

Ariella wanted to argue, to tell her husband that she didn't care whether he converted. It wasn't that her own Jewishness wasn't important to her. She never denied or denigrated her heritage, and her parents' escape from Eastern Europe on the eve of Hitler's war underlaid her very identity. She just saw no reason for Abel to involve himself with Judaism. Religion wasn't a factor in her own life; why should it be in her husband's? She had repeatedly told him as much but he continued to harp on the idea. And this didn't seem like a very good time to stake out her ground again. Abel was clearly upset.

"Ariella, conversion to a new faith isn't like going for a new college degree, is it? It doesn't make sense. Even Catholicism requires a dunking!"

"I don't know," Ariella tried to console Abel. "I think you're making things seem bigger than they really are. There's nothing wrong with you the way you are. And anyway, if you really want a Jewish identity, it does make sense to read about Judaism, doesn't it?"

"Oh, I'll read the books all right, but that won't be the end of it. I'm not going back to that rabbi. I think it's time we connected with someone more traditional."

Ariella felt a strange, sinking feeling as though a roller coaster had started moving but she really didn't want to be aboard.

"You mean a *Conservative* rabbi?" she asked nervously.

"Precisely," her husband replied.

CHAPTER 6

Uneasy Feelings

The atmosphere was as pleasant and warm as their guide was distant and cold. Standing in the kindergarten of the Louis Finkelstein Jewish School, Abel, Ariella and Rabbi Frederick Allen, the principal of the school, observed the class in session before them.

Two teachers stood in opposite corners of the room, each surrounded by several children eagerly jumping up and down with hands raised to their tiny limits. Rabbi Allen was being as accommodating as his nature allowed him, but his voice was a study in contrast to the spontaneity and life spread before them.

"We are particularly proud of our kindergarten here at the Finkelstein School. Our teachers are very capable. Would you like to talk to one of them?"

Ariella didn't feel she should disturb the women so she declined. Abel asked if he and his wife could just stay and watch for a while.

"Certainly," Rabbi Allen said. "As a matter of fact, I have some work to do, but you can just stop by my office before you leave."

"We'll do that, thank you," Abel replied.

Ariella was already busy studying the interactions between the room's human seedlings and their cultivators. Abel joined her in her concentration after the rabbi had left. The couple sat quietly for several minutes, unaware of the delicate smiles creeping across their faces.

Ariella interrupted the silence with a whisper.

"I'll tell you one thing," she said without taking her eyes off the children and their teachers.

"Rabbi Solomon at the other school was a whole lot more personable than this guy."

"Maybe Rabbi Allen is just one of those efficient kinds of people who do their jobs really well but don't come across as terribly friendly."

"Maybe so," Ariella conceded without conviction. "But it really doesn't make a difference. I like the feel of this place, or at least of this room."

The Finkelstein School was housed in one wing of the edifice of Beth Am, the largest Conservative congregation in the state. The place was overwhelming in its grandeur. Even as one approached from the outside, it commanded immediate respect: a colossus amid the Lilliputian residences of the upper-class neighborhood it honored with its presence. Though the school wing was modest by comparison, the main body of the complex seemed to ooze majesty into its every appendage. The kindergarten room, however, as Ariella had remarked, remained unpretentious and cozy.

"I guess the innocence of kids this age creates its own environment," Abel suggested.

His wife smiled and nodded in agreement.

Their eyes on the children to the last moment, the couple finally returned to Rabbi Allen's office, where they informed him of their decision to enroll their girls in the kindergarten for the coming school year. He handed them some material to read and various forms to complete and wished them well.

As they walked out into the bright, early-summer sunshine toward their car, Abel marveled at how the kindergartners were being taught Hebrew letters.

"Little kids like that," he gushed, "learning a foreign language with an entirely strange alphabet! I can't wait for the twins to start."

"I know what you mean," Ariella said as she unlocked the door. "Preschool was basically glorified babysitting, but this is real school. Our babies are going to be students!"

A wave of warmth washed over the couple and they laughed in happy anticipation.

Considerably less pleasant was the ride home from Beth Am four months later. The children had been attending the kindergarten for several weeks, Abel had made preliminary inquiries about Conservative conversion, and he and his wife were returning from their first parent-teacher open house.

During the program, Ariella had asked Rabbi Allen if the children's Hebrew word lists could include, in addition to English translations, transliterations to aid parents like herself and her husband, who didn't read Hebrew very well. She had only intended to become more involved in the twins' education, but as soon as the words had left her mouth, she sensed that Abel had been deeply embarrassed by her request. During the ride home, he quickly confirmed her hunch.

"How could you ask for transliterations?" he asked quietly but incredulously.

"Because we need them," replied Ariella, opting for clarity if not caution.

But I'm learning Hebrew!" Abel exclaimed, hurt oozing from each word.

"Abel, I know that," Ariella said. "But I just thought it would be more efficient if we had the girls' vocabulary words written out in English. And not just for you — I can't read Hebrew either! I was just trying to make things easier," she explained, drawing out the last word pointedly.

Something crystallized in Abel's mind. He had heard just the words to make him see red. The pain in his voice turned to something more like anger.

"*Easier* isn't what's important! I don't want us to have an *easy* time. I want us to be a real Jewish family, with whatever difficulties, problems and challenges any Jewish family has to handle. That rabbi who tried to sell me a reading course as a conversion was trying to make Judaism *easier*, and now so are you! Why must it be easy when it's never been easy to be Jewish — and it was never *meant* to be? I don't know how you can take things so lightly!"

Ariella knew now, if ever she had doubted it, that she had a real problem on her hands, that her husband was determined to involve Judaism in their lives. Abel's outrage at her straightforward, profoundly reasonable request of Rabbi Allen wasn't at all what it seemed. He couldn't possibly really be upset at the prospect of clearer home teaching aids, she knew. No, it was pure and simple frustration Abel was venting, the result of the clash between his desire to be truly Jewish and his inability to uncover just what that meant. This "issue," she realized, was just an excuse, a silly straw on this complex camel's back.

A chill swept over Ariella. She hadn't bargained for this. Her husband was riveted to an incomprehensible and disturbing goal. She wondered if their marriage would survive Abel's obsession. Hastily, she wiped a tear from her eye.

Meanwhile, Abel had simmered down.

"If I had wanted easy," he said quietly, "I could have been a Unitarian."

Inwardly, Ariella had to smile, though she wore her pursed lips like a mask. They'd survive, she knew. But it wouldn't be easy.

"Abel," she ventured after a few minutes, clearing her throat so she'd sound less teary, "I think it would help if, while you're discussing conversion with Rabbi Allen, we started attending services. Maybe it would help mainstream us into things."

Abel had been thinking the same thing and he mumbled his embarrassed approval.

When they arrived home, Ariella went right to the phone and called the Beth Am office to find out what time services would be held that Friday night.

Though Friday was almost a week away, it seemed to arrive within moments.

41

Dressed in their Sunday best and trying not to look as obtrusive as they felt, Abel and Ariella entered the cavernous sanctuary for Sabbath evening services, each parent holding a four-year-old's hand. The girls shimmered in identical pink, chiffon dresses.

The sanctuary — the Ignatz Cowan Sanctuary, according to the heavy, bronze plaque above its ornate doors — was the hub of the huge Beth Am complex, though it was only used for Friday night and Saturday morning services. Various other studies and offices sufficed for the less attended weekday morning services. Afternoon services were held only on special occasions.

As the family of first-time congregants entered the sanctuary, they were struck by its relentless ambience, which lay somewhere between a fin de siècle opera house and a medieval version of the heavenly palace. As if to emphasize the grandeur of the surroundings, the commanding presence of a magnificent dome overhead seemed to threaten the mortals dwarfed beneath it. The sanctuary was no less stunning to the ears than to the eyes, for the cantor's chanting reverberated impressively throughout the room. Abel noticed a sophisticated speaker system assisting the cantorials but the place's acoustics were undeniably superb.

Ariella imagined the cantor as a young Charleton Heston but when she finally got a distant look at him, he was unmistakably squat and bald. His voice, though, with the help of the acoustics and the speakers, was overpowering.

Abel and Ariella took seats in the middle of the sanctuary rather than at the fringes, lest they exacerbate their uncomfortable sense of newness and impede their integration into the gathering of worshippers. They were resolved to experience the service to the fullest, with minimal self-consciousness, despite Abel's dark skin and the fact that he hadn't yet converted. The twins sat on their parents' laps, curiously eyeing the big theater. They had many questions to ask but, not knowing quite where to begin and feeling rather tired for the late hour, they remained silent.

Just as the foursome had begun to relax and the feeling of several hundred pairs of eyes focused on them had subsided, the first part of the service ended abruptly. The last echo of the cantor's voice gave way to a deep silence punctuated only by a surprisingly amplified cough or two. It was time, the couple realized after a moment's uncertainty, for the rabbi's sermon.

Rabbi Shoman, Beth Am's senior rabbi, had penetrating eyes, impeccably coiffed hair and an uncanny resemblance to a young Jimmy Swaggart. This resemblance had cost him dearly in recent years, he often mused bitterly to himself, imagining the respect that would be his were he more evocative of, say, Paul Newman. But he tried to heed his own favorite sermon, accepting what he could not change, though he did endeavor to compensate for his handicap with a vocal commitment to a multitude of popular political causes. The media people knew to call him immediately for an authoritative rabbinical comment, and photographs of his good, somewhat less Swaggarty side were commonplace in the local papers.

Rabbi Shoman rose from his seat on the dais, as he did every Friday night, and strode with slow, deliberate confidence to the podium just in front of the holy ark.

Just then, Abel turned to his wife.

"Look around, dear. Do you notice anything about the other congregants?" he whispered quickly.

"Uh, yes," Ariella whispered back. "Nobody else has kids with them."

Abel was about to speculate further on the observation but the rabbi had begun to speak. The sermon was about Nicaraguan rebels, and though Abel tried to pay attention, the rabbi's words couldn't hold him. Glancing at Ariella, Abel saw a look of total disinterest on her face. The couple's boredom was soon replaced by acute embarrassment, however. The twins had dozed off and were snoring loudly, as they always did when they slept.

In any other environment, the snoring would have barely been noticeable, but in the Ignatz Cowan Sanctuary, the unsynchronized cadences seemed to strike the dome overhead and bounce back even louder. The amplified snoring resonated through the cavernous hall, the resulting cacophony competing with the rabbi's eloquent defense of Sandinista political philosophy.

Ariella labored desperately to shake Ruth awake but Abel didn't even try with Daphna. He knew it was futile; the twins slept like hibernating bears.

"What'll we DO?" Areilla whispered loudly to her husband as they noticed full faces in their periphery where earlier there had been only profiles.

To stand up and leave in the middle of the rabbi's sermon would have been an even greater embarrassment. The pews were full and the closest aisle was a dozen worshippers away. The twins were hopeless, so the new parishioners just took deep breaths, stared straight at the rabbi with feigned attention, and imagined themselves elsewhere. As the blathering and whistling of the slumbering twins punctuated the list of terrorized Nicaraguan towns the rabbi had begun to catalogue, Abel imagined the combined sounds as some delirious, drunken mariachi band.

In several minutes, mercifully, the ordeal was over. As the rabbi reached his seat, the cantor led the congregation in one final song, and then services were over.

The crowd spilled out of the sanctuary and filed past Rabbis Shoman and Allen, who smiled and shook hands with their congregants. Abel and Ariella, each shouldering a still-snoring twin, dutifully joined the line.

If Rabbi Shoman harbored any ill will toward them for bringing the girls along, he hid it well. His smile and "Shabbat shalom" were the same for the Gomes family as for everyone before them in line. In fact, the smile seemed almost fixed, the greeting recorded.

The laden couple then moved on to Rabbi Allen, who extended a more subdued greeting. As they were about to step away from him into the safety of the world beyond the sanctuary, the clergyman seemed to want to say something more, so Abel and Ariella lingered for a moment.

Rabbi Allen hesitated, and then awkwardly but politely said, "Perhaps Saturday morning services might be a better time for you folks to bring your children."

Ariella looked him coldly in the eye and thanked him for his suggestion.

CHAPTER 7

Conservative Ties

Abel and Ariella did return to Beth Am for Saturday morning services with their children. And often on Friday nights without them. Eventually, people stopped staring at the newcomers and friendships developed. For several months, Abel seemed content with the degree of affiliation he and Ariella had achieved.

Ariella, for her part, was relieved at the reasonable amount of religion her husband had brought into their lives. While it was hardly a meal in a five-star restaurant, the Friday night service did offer her an opportunity to get out of the house and spend time with her husband in a place where the phone couldn't ring and no chores beckoned. Neither the service nor the sermons particularly touched her, but she didn't really mind them. With her husband beside her and the hundreds of other couples seated around them, the feel of the place was pleasant, almost romantic. She imagined the pews floating in some Venetian canal, the cantor a gondolier.

"I think I'm ready to convert," Abel announced one morning without warning after the girls had been picked up for school.

Ariella felt the sticky spray of her burst bubble.

"I think you're ready to go to work," she countered with droll disregard.

"I've still got twenty minutes," Abel replied, unruffled, "and I wanted to hear how you felt about my decision."

"Do what you want."

The terseness hit Abel squarely.

"Don't you care?" he asked.

The thought had welled up within her more often than she cared to remember in recent months, and now she felt it rise again from somewhere deep. This time, it didn't stall in her throat.

"If I had wanted a Jewish husband, Abel, I would have married one."

There was an awkward silence as Abel tried desperately to climb out from under his wife's words.

"Does that mean you don't want one?" he finally managed.

"I don't *need* one, Abel. That's all I'm saying."

Abel gathered his thoughts and, after a moment, spoke.

"Ariella, there was a time when I wanted to be Jewish because of you, for your sake and for the girls. But I'm not doing it now because of you, though you're always my connection to Judaism. I'm doing it because I, because I..." he groped for words. "Because I should be! Because *we* should be!"

He couldn't have chosen less reassuring words for Ariella. For some time now, she had felt threatened by her husband's gravitation toward her heritage. She was especially apprehensive about what impact it would have on her own life and happiness. Ariella feared it would force her into a lifestyle she didn't want. She didn't need restrictions on what she ate or how she spent her time. She didn't want conversations about theology or social causes. She had no desire for some rabbi to shove an outdated, if spruced up, patriarchal faith down her throat.

And here Abel wanted not only to take it all on himself but to impose it on her! Somehow, she held her anger in check and tried to conduct a cool, logical discussion.

"But Abel, everything's fine the way it is. The kids are in a good Jewish school, we attend services regularly, we're making friends. What's the problem? Why can't you be satisfied with things as they are?"

Abel didn't answer. He lacked the words to describe the unripe feeling, the sense of incompleteness that had plagued him for what seemed an eternity. He couldn't recall ever caring that Ariella was Jewish back when they were dating, yet recently he had begun to suspect that even part of his motivation in marrying her had come from some inscrutable desire to connect with Judaism. Now he felt an overwhelming and equally inexplicable urge to take another step. His wife — part of him — was Jewish. He wanted the rest of him to follow.

But Abel couldn't think of how to say it all, at least not without sounding patronizing toward Ariella — or downright crazy.

"Ariella," he began, "it's not that I'm dissatisfied, at least not in the sense you mean. It's just that a person has to keep growing, pursuing his ideals and goals, and being Jewish is my goal. You've always taken pride in your own Jewishness, so how can you deny me my own desire to be Jewish like you?"

"I'm sorry, Abel, but my pride is in my parents and grandparents, in their lives and their survival of the Nazis. It's not a religious thing. I don't need laws and rituals and garbage like that. I'm an intelligent, modern person, for heaven's sake! And so are you! Why can't you take pride in your own heritage — the Cape Verdean community has such a rich culture and your grandmother's an American Indian *princess*, for goodness sake! — and just live your own life in the twentieth century?"

Abel realized it wouldn't suffice to use the word "heritage" when he really meant much more, however it might prejudice his wife against him.

"There's more to life than ethnic pride. I'm proud of my Portuguese and Narragansett roots. But I never felt any desire to practice my grandmother's religion when I went to powwows and tribal meetings. Something's pulling me toward your religion, though."

There. He had said the "R word." He tried not to miss a beat, hoping to avoid Ariella's immediate response.

"I can't explain it," he continued, "but something inside me is moving me in that direction and I feel I'd be ignoring destiny if I pretend it's not real. I feel like my soul has been sort of wandering and it can finally smell the smells of home."

Abel frowned, realizing that in his haste he had indeed sounded crazy. The look on Ariella's face confirmed as much, even as she coolly reminded him that he was already late for work.

As he drove to his office, he forced himself to face the fact that he alone would be responsible for his progress toward Judaism. He couldn't expect his wife to pursue his conversion for him even if she *did* understand his desire for it, which she didn't.

As soon as Abel got to work, he called Rabbi Allen for an appointment. "To discuss conversion," he told the telephone quietly but clearly.

Rabbi Allen rose from his seat as Abel entered his office several days later, warmly shaking his guest's hand. Abel felt that the rabbi was trying too hard to seem friendly but he knew his intentions were good. He took the seat he was offered.

"So you think you're ready for conversion!" Rabbi Allen said with emphatic cheeriness.

"Well, yes, I've been considering it for quite a while and I feel there is really nothing I should be waiting for. I'm as ready as I'll ever be. I'm afraid I'm not very familiar with the procedure in Conservative Judaism, though. I once discussed conversion with a Reform rabbi, but the procedure he described really wasn't any procedure at all."

Yes, they do like to cut corners," the rabbi said in a disapproving, confidential tone. "They give liberal Judaism a bad name. We're forever chiding them to shape up and include more ritual, to help preserve true Jewish tradition, but they just don't seem to care —"

"What *is* the procedure at Beth Am?" Abel interrupted.

"Uh, yes," Rabbi Allen acknowledged his digression, "our procedure is precisely what it has always been in Judaism: immersion in the ritual bath, or *mikvah*, and, in the case of a man, circumcision."

"I'm already circumcised," Abel noted hopefully.

"Well, in that case, tradition requires that a symbolic drop of blood be drawn as sort of a reenactment of circumcision. Our cantor, an experienced *mohel*, performs the ritual and it is virtually painless."

"When can the procedure be done?" he asked quietly.

"Well, Abel," Rabbi Allen said, "first we need to set up weekly meetings to discuss various aspects of Judaism. You'll also need to read some books, which will serve as the basis for our weekly discussions. After a few months, I imagine, we'll feel that you're ready to undergo conversion."

The months passed quickly and the meetings, classes really, were informative and helpful. But Abel wasn't satisfied with a weekly connection to his goal. He read whatever book he could find about Judaism, and discussed the religion with anyone knowledgeable.

Ariella tolerated her husband's increased involvement with things Jewish and even read one or two of the books that seemed to be sprouting like mushrooms around the house, but she tried not to talk about the impending conversion or anything particularly Jewish. Abel was like a locomotive in his determination; she just stayed clear of the tracks.

When the day of his conversion arrived, Abel felt both confident and excited. Scheduled to arrive at Rabbi Shoman's office at 3:00, he was sitting impatiently in the reception area at 2:30. He watched as Rabbi Allen arrived, then another rabbi from a Conservative congregation in another city, and finally the cantor-cum-mohel. Finally, shortly after 3:00, Abel was invited inside.

As Abel entered the posh office, Rabbi Shoman directed him to a chair. He then introduced the rabbi from out of town, who, together with Beth Am's two rabbis, would constitute a *beit din*, or Jewish court, as required by Jewish law. Abel nodded and a long silence ensued. The five men fidgeted in their seats and the squeak of their bodies rubbing against the leather furniture seemed deafening. After what seemed like years, Rabbi Allen spoke.

"Well," he announced, "why don't we start?"

The cantor produced a black doctor's bag, from which he harvested a small scalpel. Abel hadn't given much thought to whether he should watch the procedure, but he decided at that moment to turn away until it was over.

He felt a cold hand touch his skin and then a slight pinch. One of the rabbis announced that the *hatafat dam brit*, or symbolic drawing of circumcision blood, was completed. Abel looked to see the blood but saw none. The cantor-*mohel*, he realized, must have stanched the small cut as soon as he had made it.

"Now we proceed to the *mikvah*," Rabbi Shoman told Abel.

It was a short drive to the unassuming and unmarked, brick building that housed the *mikvah*. Abel knew from his reading that the ritual bath was used routinely by observant Jewish women as well as for conversions. Women, he had read, used the *mikvah* at night; only conversions took place during daylight hours. Consequently, the building was deserted, save the three rabbis and Abel.

Abel lost no time preparing for what he couldn't help but think of as his Jewish baptism. Standing there naked before the clergymen, he tried to connect with generations of Jews and feel himself stripping away his own goyishness, but all he could muster was embarrassment.

Rabbi Allen motioned him to the ritual pool and Abel walked down the steps into the clear, warm water. When he was in up to his neck, he looked to see if the rabbis were watching him as required. Satisfied that they were, he let his head go under. He stayed submerged for a long time, relishing the water's protection from the six staring eyes.

When he finally came up for air, Rabbi Allen held out a towel for him and he got dressed. Then, the rabbis led him to a room and the four men sat down. Rabbi Shoman addressed Abel.

"We now need only hear your feelings for the religion you are adopting. I know you've been studying for many weeks and you have been a good student. We want to hear your own understanding of Judaism, what it means to you."

Abel tried to articulate his feelings, but words did little justice to what lay in his heart. He spoke of God but felt he sounded trite. However, when he spoke of mitzvot, the commandments of Jewish law, he thought he did a pretty good job of conveying their meaning in Judaism as he had understood it from the many books he had read.

Abel described how the moral and ethical teachings of Judaism were not thought experiments, how they required action for their realization and rabbinical guidance for their execution. The mitzvot, he said with conviction, were the very embodiment<%0> of all that Judaism stood for, and their performance was the essence of Jewish life.

He felt good having said it all, and he felt relieved and accomplished, too — something like the way he had felt as a teenager after confession. He was trying to squelch the comparison in his mind when Rabbi Shoman, making little effort to hide his irritation, interrupted him.

"Mr. Gomes," he said firmly, "what is in a Jew's heart is most important. Actions, especially of the ritual sort, are valuable only insofar as they bring one to a deeper recognition of his mission in life. You seem to have absorbed a notion that is foreign to our understanding of Conservative Judaism here at Beth Am, namely that ritual acts, even those with no meaning to modern man, have some transcendent importance of their own. Mitzvot are, of course, very important to Judaism, but they are not its mainstay. And what mitzvot a Jew undertakes to observe, and how he intends to observe them, is something best left to the individual.

"Furthermore, true Judaism does not have spiritual leaders telling their congregants what they must do or not do. Judaism is very much a personal religion, and observance a private matter between the Jew and God."

Abel was taken aback. He felt as if he had inadvertently insulted the rabbi, yet he had only expressed how he felt and what he had learned about Judaism. He was sorry that his words had been somehow objectionable. There was no doubt in his mind that Judaism *was* defined by actions, by the commandments of the Torah, and that rabbis were to help people perform these commandments.

Abel remembered how, just several months before, he had read a book that, like Rabbi Shoman, had stressed attitude, emotion and a sense of mission and commitment to human growth and a better world as the essentials of Judaism. It didn't even mention commandments or requirements. "You know, Ariella," he had snickered to his wife, "if this is all there is to Judaism, I'm *already* Jewish!"

But he'd known even then that the book was a joke. Abel had learned enough about Judaism from more cogent sources, and had thought enough about life and Jewish history, to know that a Divine revelation at Sinai and the permanence of the Biblical commandments were the true hallmarks of Judaism. And he knew that was precisely why he didn't really feel Jewish, and why he needed to convert according to Jewish law.

And here, the very rabbi converting him was chiding him for overemphasizing mitzvot. It was all so very confusing.

Well, at least he was now legally Jewish, he assured himself.

Abel realized that the rabbi was still talking, now about how modern Jewish identity was synonymous with perpetuating the memory of the Holocaust. It might have been some ancient Iberian ghost stirring inside him, but Abel couldn't help but wonder why the persecution of the Jews in the Middle Ages, or, for that matter, at the time of Titus or Hadrian, held no similar significance for Rabbi Shoman.

Abel nodded politely and reminded the rabbi that his in-laws were Eastern European survivors so he had, in a way, "married" into the Holocaust. The rabbi seemed pleased.

"Have you chosen a Hebrew name, Mr. Gomes?" Rabbi Allen asked.

Abel had.

"I want to take the name Ovadyah," he informed the court, giving the Hebrew pronunciation of the prophet Obadiah, "who was born a non-Jew like I was and converted."

None of those present had been aware of the rabbinic tradition that the prophet Ovadyah had descended from Esau — Jacob's antithetical brother — but they smiled anyway and nodded sagely, content to allow their new convert his well-researched caprice.

CHAPTER 8

Diminishing Returns

Ariella took Abel's conversion in stride. Her fears for her marriage and sanity had subsided somewhat, in proportion to her husband's lessening frustration. As Abel had anticipated his upcoming rite of passage, he had felt distinctly relieved, and his happier demeanor had allowed Ariella a new perspective: her husband wasn't crazy, she realized, just determined.

So mellow had she become that she hesitated only briefly when Abel asked her to get married again.

As their marriage had never been a Jewish one, Rabbi Shoman felt that they should renew their commitment to one another. A ceremony was scheduled for several days later.

With the couple's immediate family in attendance, the marriage was quickly performed in Rabbi Shoman's office. The rabbi intoned some Hebrew phrases, Ovadyah was shown what to say, and the couple was declared husband and wife. Not bad, thought Ovadyah afterward: he'd become both a Jew and a newlywed in the same week.

After the ceremony, Ovadyah and Ariella dropped the girls off at home with a sitter and went out to a kosher deli to celebrate. The pastrami was good, but no better, Ovadyah had to admit, than when his taste buds had been gentile. Still, he felt much better about himself now that his conversion was behind him.

As the two finished their meal, each lost in thought, it suddenly struck Ovadyah that he was not the only one enjoying the repast from a new perspective. He had noticed a change in Ariella's attitude, too, which had evolved slowly over the weeks before his conversion. Whereas the past had mostly seen her oppose her husband's growth in Judaism, she had recently grown gradually but unmistakably supportive. He was curious.

"Listen, Ariella, I want you to know that it's meant everything to me that you've been behind me in all this."

"As of late," Ariella pointed out with a bit of self-derision.

"Better late than never," he said with a sheepish, knowing smile.

"Abel — "

"Ovadyah," he corrected.

She laughed along with him.

"Ovadyah, dear," she began again, "I want you to know that I'm with you."

"I know, I feel it."

"You probably wonder what changed."

"Well, come to mention it..." Ovadyah let his sentence dangle.

"I've been wondering myself," Ariella confessed. "Believe it or not, though I've tried and tried, I can't put my finger on it. I just can't remember any event or conversation that really turned me around. Maybe I just finally realized that it really was what you wanted, and that was all I needed. I don't know."

"Who cares what did it? As long as you're happy with your Jewish husband."

Ovadyah smiled broadly but Ariella didn't notice. She was still deep in thought, her eyes glued to her plate.

"It really is strange, though," she continued. "Once I became convinced that you were actually going through with this, my frustrations began to ebb. I just couldn't hold on to a gripe. Everything that happened from that point on seemed to make me want to help you. I even found myself starting to *think* like you!"

"Uh oh," Ovadyah sympathized.

"No, I mean it," Ariella went on. "Like when we started keeping Shabbat: When you first brought up the idea of your `practicing' Sabbath observance before your conversion, I was surprised at how anxious I was to try things out."

Only several months earlier, they had undertaken to observe the Jewish Sabbath in all its detail, refraining not only from work of the obvious sort but from sundry activities like driving, cooking and writing. Ariella's cooperation had been an unexpected blessing, but Ovadyah hadn't wanted to look a gift horse in the mouth so he had never asked her about it.

"I actually found myself just as obsessed with the laws and technicalities of observance as you were," Ariella marveled. "Remember when I was reading that cutesy book, the one that read like an abridged encyclopedia of Jewish life through the eyes of an aging flower child?"

"*The Jewish Catalogue*?" Ovadyah ventured.

"That's it. Well, I remember reading about Shabbat and its restful, peaceful atmosphere, about the beauty and warmth of the day and the festive meals. It was all really lovely. But suddenly I started feeling almost *angry* at the book. I didn't want to know how I'd *feel* about the Sabbath, I wanted to know how to *do* it. I was thinking like you!"

"My sympathies," Ovadyah said drolly, but he felt deeply at one with his wife. As they laughed together, Ovadyah felt a tear of indeterminate origin in his eye.

The next day, as Ovadyah had arranged, Rabbi Allen came to the house to survey the kitchen and provide some rabbinical guidance in making it kosher.

Ariella was at work, which Ovadyah thought was just as well; she'd been great so far but he worried that the intrusion on her kitchen might be a bit too much for her. He knew that complicated criteria governed which pots, pans, dishes and cutlery were "kasherable" and which were hopelessly non-kosher. Even the oven and stovetop would need treatment, and though Ovadyah had a good idea of just what would be required, he had felt that Rabbi Allen's imprimatur would make him and Ariella more secure that their home was indeed kosher.

"Well," the rabbi informed him after being given the royal tour of the Gomes kitchen, "the porcelain will have to go."

Ovadyah had known as much but it felt good to hear the rabbi confirm his research.

"Everything else," Rabbi Allen continued, "can stay."

"And what do I need to do to it all?" Ovadyah asked.

"Just wash it well."

"And then?"

"And *then*? And then *use* it, Abel."

"Ovadyah," Ovadyah corrected. "I meant, what do I have to do in terms of kashering it?"

"Nothing. Just clean the oven and dishes well and, of course, keep using kosher food."

"You mean I don't have to dip any of the pots into boiling water or blowtorch the oven walls or any of that stuff?" Ovadyah inquired, recalling some of the things he had read.

"Uh, I don't think anything so drastic will be necessary," the rabbi said, trying not to sound as sorry as he felt for his earnest congregant.

Ovadyah thought he detected a hint of condescension in the rabbi's voice but he wrote it off to the clergyman's generally subdued demeanor. He thanked his visitor for the advice he had provided and saw him to the door.

That evening, when he shared the details of Rabbi Allen's visit with Ariella, she reacted with the same surprise.

"He knew what we had used the pots and things for?" she asked incredulously.
"I told him," Ovadyah insisted.

Ariella thought for a moment before speaking.

"Why don't we just do what the books on *kashrut* require?"

Ovadyah couldn't have scripted a better line for his wife. They got right to work boiling up a large pot of water. Using a pair of tongs, they proceeded to immerse their smaller pots, pans and cutlery in the steaming brew.

It was hard, sweaty work and not without its hazards, as several burns on Ovadyah and Ariella's hands bore witness. But when it was over, they beamed with a feeling of accomplishment, and that night they slept an unusually deep, rejuvenating sleep.

The next morning, Ovadyah phoned Rabbi Allen with his second question of Jewish law, which he had forgotten to ask the day before. Not wanting to impugn the propriety of the rabbi's own suggestions, he made sure not to mention the previous night's kashering session. And when he broached the new subject, he well realized the wisdom of his omission.

"Rabbi, I'm sorry to bother you, but I'm about to buy a new suit and I wanted to check on the procedure."

The silence on the other end of the line was born of utter bewilderment. Finally, it ended.

"The procedure? Uh, well, one goes to a store and, uh, looks for one's size, I suppose."

Ovadyah's hearty laugh cut the rabbi short.

"That's cute," he said between guffaws, though Rabbi Allen had not been trying to be. He never tried to be cute.

"I'm afraid I don't understand you," he finally said bluntly.

Somewhat taken aback, Ovadyah explained what he had assumed the rabbi knew.

"Well, I've heard that linen is used in certain areas of woolen suits."

"Yes?" Rabbi Allen replied, awaiting further information.

"Isn't there a Biblical prohibition against wearing a garment containing wool and linen?"

Ovadyah asked hesitantly.

Finally, Rabbi Allen sighed to himself, *a clue to what was on this odd convert's mind.*

"Well, yes, there is a verse in the Torah concerning that," he said patiently.

"So I wanted to know," Ovadyah continued, "how I could tell which suits have linen in them and which don't. I mean, I know the labels don't tell you what's in the lining and collar underlining, so are there certain types to avoid? Or is there anyone locally who can test a garment for linen content?"

Ovadyah knew that in many cities there were trained testers for "*shaatnez*," as the forbidden mixture of wool and linen was called, though he didn't know of anyone in the area. He figured the rabbi would know.

The rabbi didn't know. He took a deep breath before he spoke.

"Mr. Gomes — "

"Please call me by my first name, Rabbi," Ovadyah interjected cheerfully.

"Abel — " the rabbi began again.

"Ovadyah," the telephone corrected.

"Ovadyah," the rabbi repeated, revealing a hint of his exasperation, "we don't observe that law today."

Ovadyah struggled to comprehend the rabbi's words. A blunter response than he would have consciously formulated emerged from his mouth.

"It's in the Torah," he said simply.

"Yes, well, it certainly is. But many things in the Torah represent the times in which they were written. The varied perceptions of the Torah's authors, too, are apparent in different places. Not all the laws within the Torah are necessarily pertinent to modern man, you realize."

Ovadyah had realized nothing of the sort. For him, it was a revelation — so to speak — that the rabbi felt that way.

"So you're saying that you don't observe the prohibition of wearing wool and linen in a garment?"

"Put it this way," Rabbi Allen responded, trying to project a voice of reason, "when I find some meaning to the law, then I'll consider observing it."

Ovadyah really wanted to ascertain the rabbi's conception of the Torah. His own clearly included the facts of its Divine origin and the immutability of its laws, despite their inscrutability. These tenets had always constituted the very basis of Jewish belief through the ages, Ovadyah had understood from his reading. But he decided a theological discussion would be better left for another time, so he thanked Rabbi Allen for his help and hung up.

Reflecting on what he had learned — about the rabbi's beliefs, if not about Jewish law — he felt a mixture of irritation and amusement. The feelings didn't belong together, he realized, but there they were just the same. He tried to describe them to Ariella later that day.

"When I was on the phone, I felt like I'd stumbled into the `bein hashemashot zone,'" he quipped.

"The who?"

"'*Bein hashemashot*' is Hebrew for `twilight,'" he explained, proud to display a new bit of vocabulary he'd culled from a book about the Sabbath in Jewish law. "It's really bizarre when you think about it: rabbis without Judaism."

Suddenly and frantically, his eyebrows shot up and he began looking about the room, behind the door, under the couch. Suspecting one of her usually staid husband's occasional crazy routines, Ariella tried not to smile.

"What *are* you doing, dear?"

"Looking for Rod Serling. I'll bet he's behind the drapes."

Ariella's smile pushed itself through and she remembered why she had married the man who now stood before her, feet slightly apart, hands folded in front of him. She knew what was coming.

"Little did Ovadyah and Ariella realize," he began, with a nasal voice, squinted eyes and a cocky jerk of his head, "that Judaism isn't really Judaism and rabbis aren't really rabbis. At least not where *they* had ventured. Not in...the *bein hashemashot* zone!"

Ariella did the sound effects and the couple had a good laugh milking Rabbi Allen's responses to their queries. But their underlying uneasiness remained.

CHAPTER 9

Different Strokes

The Conservative movement, Ovadyah and Ariella found, allowed generous latitude in belief and observance. While some of their friends in the congregation ate kosher food exclusively, others kept kosher homes but would eat out in non-kosher restaurants. To such people, *kashrut* was only a symbolic statement and therefore didn't demand constant adherence. Many others at Beth Am made no effort at all to keep kosher, relegating the realm of the Jewish dietary laws to that of *shaatnez* in Rabbi Allen's world view.

The Sabbath was similarly acknowledged by members of the synagogue. Some saw the day simply as an opportunity to relax in the American sense of the word. They didn't consider services particularly recreational so they opted for movies, picnics or just staying home to watch television or wash their cars. For others, a Sabbath without services was as unthinkable as Monday night without football, so Friday night found them sitting in Beth Am's pews. Still, the ancient Sabbath laws held little importance for them, and once services were over, the day was just another piece of the weekend.

Several members of the congregation took things more seriously, however. While they, too, would never dream of treating Shabbat with the picayune stringency of the Orthodox — who could barely breathe without some sabbatical restriction — they felt that the Jewish Sabbath's laws helped define the essence of the day. These congregants not only attended services but ate the requisite festive meals in honor of the day. They also refrained from non-Jewish distractions, like sports events or movies. Most would drive on the Sabbath, a violation of the law prohibiting all types of combustion, but the Conservative movement had long since permitted driving to synagogue on the Sabbath, so the automobile had effectively lost its Sabbath stigma for most Conservative Jews.

Nevertheless, Ovadyah and Ariella decided that the traditional Jewish laws of the Sabbath were too important, historically and conceptually, to be pushed aside for mere convenience's — or conformance's — sake. So while their fellow congregants overwhelmingly considered driving, cooking and other technical violations of Sabbath law to be conventions of little or no consequence, Ovadyah and Ariella felt that while the peaceful and restful spirit of the law might well complement its letter, it could never replace it.

So it was that they opted for what was, among their friends, a somewhat unusual Sabbath. Though they did drive the several miles to Beth Am, following the directive of the Conservative rabbinate, once they arrived home again they considered the car off-limits. Their Sabbath day was spent at home, resting and enjoying special meals that consisted of precooked or cold food. And they did their best to avoid any other violations of traditional Jewish Sabbath law.

The same seriousness they displayed in their religious observance, they applied with equal vigor to synagogue responsibilities. Within a year of their first visit to Beth Am, both Ovadyah and Ariella had undertaken important positions within its religious and educational structure.

As the director of the adult education program, Ovadyah arranged night classes on varied Jewish subjects for interested synagogue members and potential converts. He had also been given the considerable honor of the position of *gabbai*, or sexton, the person who oversees the prayer services and ensures that the different roles therein — the leader of the services, the reader of the Torah, and those called to say the blessing over it — are distributed equitably and executed properly. Insofar as these roles are assigned largely at the *gabbai*'s discretion, the position entails a certain prominence and is usually reserved for someone thoroughly trustworthy and familiar with synagogue procedure.

Ovadyah had arrived. By electing him gabbai, his fellow congregants had affirmed his sincerity, dedication and abilities. He had earned the respect of his peers, and while he was not one to revel in personal glory, he was proud to serve such an important function.

Ariella, for her part, had become equally recognized for her own dedication and talent. As president of the Louis Finkelstein Jewish School's Parent-Teacher Association, she made important decisions regarding the workings and direction of the school.

There was little doubt that the name Gomes had become a respected one at Beth Am. Both Ovadyah and Ariella felt comfortable there and fully accepted. Ovadyah's coloration seemed of little concern to anyone, and while it did more or less indicate that he was a "Jew by choice" — the "in" expression for converts at Beth Am — there were so many others in the congregation that it was hardly a handicap. Once, though, several months after Ovadyah's appointment as *gabbai*, he and Ariella had attended a social function at Beth Am and a rather loud, middle-aged woman had tried to get his attention from across the room by yelling, "Hey, Chiquito!" with a linebacker's gusto. But Ovadyah had felt more embarrassed for her than insulted, especially when others near the Amazon immediately turned her into a puddle of shame with their outraged stares.

The only other time Ovadyah's racial background had been, if indirectly, treated with condescension was when another woman in the congregation confided to Ariella, "Your husband is so handsome, so well-groomed, so polite and intelligent, I can really understand why you married him!" as if were it not for his exemplary qualities, there would have been less reason to marry him than any of the less endowed husbands in the congregation. Ariella was mortified to realize the woman's state of mind but, knowing how Ovadyah would want her to ignore the faint praise, she held her tongue and even managed a passably gracious smile.

All in all, though, Beth Am offered warm friendships and room for personal growth, not to mention opportunities galore for socializing with other Jews and learning more about Judaism. One opportunity the couple found particularly exciting, as it combined human interaction with intellectual and spiritual growth, was the chance to join a *chavurah*.

Back in the '60s, the Conservative leadership discovered that much of the movement's membership tended to reserve their synagogues and rabbis for special occasions rather than viewing them as spiritual lodes to be mined regularly. To deal with this mentality, a brilliant idea was conceived: If people could not be coaxed into orbiting their lives around beautiful and inviting houses of worship, the reasoning went, maybe a more religious and Judaically educational environment could be created in the home itself, bringing the mountain to Mohammed, so to speak.

Cynical Orthodox folk pointed out at the time that Jewish education and observance would never have left the Jewish home in the first place had the non-Orthodox movements not sanctioned the abandonment of traditional Jewish law. But the Conservative rabbinate had long since inured itself to the jealous jibes of less enlightened Jews and ignored all such noises from "the right."

So, sensing a golden opportunity to awaken interest in Conservatism as something more than a way out of Orthodoxy's stringencies, Conservative rabbis encouraged their congregants to form small groups and meet, weekly or monthly, at each other's homes to discuss Jewish affairs, study Jewish texts, listen to speakers or just talk about life. The idea spread like a revolution; it seemed to supply precisely that combination of religion and reality that had somehow never flourished in the sanctuaries and libraries of the Conservative movement. *Chavurot*, as the groups were called, sprung up throughout the country.

There were several *chavurot* within the Beth Am membership and Rabbi Allen directed the Gomeses to one that included other Sabbath-service attendees with children in the Finkelstein School. Ovadyah and Ariella were excited to participate in what promised to be not only an educational experience but an important element in the rejuvenation of Conservative Judaism.

The *chavurah* met each Shabbat and occasionally on holidays. Five couples all told, they were a serious, eclectic group and their discussions ranged from politics to recipes to Halachah, or Jewish law.

All the members were well aware that Jewish law had held Judaism together since its beginnings, but they were confident that Halachah reflected the attitudes and assumptions of men (and *not* women) far removed from the present. Conservatism appealed to these couples precisely because it insisted that Halachah had to remain timely in order to survive into the Jewish future.

Indeed, one of the chavurah's first acts had been to ask Rabbi Shoman a modern question of Jewish law. As their get-togethers were held Friday nights or Saturday afternoons, and as the Conservative movement had only sanctioned driving on the Sabbath to attend services, the members of the group wanted to know if they could drive to their *chavurah* meetings.

The rabbi had answered, with a benevolent smile, that their camaraderie was undoubtedly more important than any mere technicality, and that not only was driving to the meetings permitted, it was a "mitzvah," a good deed. Though Rabbi Shoman'sresponse to their second question, concerning whether the chavurah should hold its own Sabbath services in its members' homes, had been somewhat less encouraging, they were happy with his directive regarding driving on the Sabbath and thanked him for his help.

On the eve of their first *chavurah* meeting, Ovadyah and Ariella came up against a slight problem. Since certain members of the chavurah didn't keep kosher, the couple realized they would not be able to eat the food served at some of the gatherings. They could, they considered, simply not eat when attending a meeting at those members' homes, but refreshments were a major part of the evenings' social interaction and they knew they'd feel like lepers if their mouths were the only empty ones. Ovadyah wondered whether their hosts might be insulted if they brought their own victuals, but Ariella pointed out that no offense could conceivably be taken. "After all," she asked, "why should a religious need be any less compelling than, say, a medical need?" So the couple decided to adhere to their standards of *kashrut* and hope for the best. What they got, though, was something considerably less.

"What are you trying to do? Make a statement or something?" queried one scarlet-faced woman when the Gomeses arrived at the first meeting with Tupperware in hand. The hosts, too, seemed offended by the foreign food, though they kept their thoughts to themselves.

Ariella tried to defuse the social dynamite encased in the green, plastic bowl by explaining how insignificant it was that she had brought special food for herself and her husband in light of the closeness they felt for their chavurah comrades in the more fundamental realms beyond the culinary. Ovadyah added with a smile that there were different levels of kashrut observance. Choosing one, he said, did not necessitate looking down on the choosers of others.

All to little avail. The umbrageous attendant fumed throughout the meeting, casting stares at the Gomeses that could have frozen fire. The situation was helped little by the fact that the evening's subject was "Halachah in Daily Life." The discussion began in the areas of Sabbath observance and gender roles but quickly migrated, despite the attempts of some considerate members, to matters of the kitchen.

Ovadyah tried to steer the discussion away from the earlier Tupperware exchange and keep it in the more placid realm of the theoretical.

"Well," he argued, "the Bible itself forbids the eating of certain species, and the halachic literature clearly requires a particular way of slaughtering even the permitted animals. And Jews have separated between meat and milk foods since time immemorial."

"But Ovadyah," one of the evening's hosts interjected, "shouldn't we be discussing not what the Halachah *has been* but what it *should be*? In other words, do we really need the dietary laws altogether these days?"

Ovadyah was taken aback. He had well understood that the Conservative philosophy was dedicated to the evolution and modernization of Jewish law, but he never thought an entire area of Halachah could be shed like a shirt on a muggy day.

Ariella, sharing his surprise, spoke up.

"Where would you draw the line? I mean, declare this law primitive, that one no longer meaningful, the other out of sync with modern society — why not just start a new religion from scratch?"

Her words crawled like ants over her listeners' skin. The *chavurah* members fidgeted and grimaced as they searched for the right response to Ariella's outrageous suggestion.

"Judaism's essence has always been its social conscience," one finally said, "and no one is considering altering that in any way."

"You might not know it," interjected another, "but Jewish law has been updated repeatedly since ancient times!"

"Maybe you'd like to advocate Orthodoxy," the woman who had been so outraged at the Gomeses' food containers sneered, "and then next week you can bring some stones for us to throw at each other!"

At that, several members interceded to defend, if not agree with, the besieged couple, standing up for the Gomeses' right to eat what they pleased, though some of them, remembering that the chavurah was to meet at everyone's home sooner or later, felt pangs of resentment at the thought of the plastic containers on their own dining-room tables.

That particular get-together left an odd taste in the mouths of all present, but their mutual dedication to the *chavurah* kept the weekly meetings going. Those hosts who made no effort to observe the dietary laws — or to hide the fact — had to endure the rusticity of guests appearing with food in tow. The resultant tension notwithstanding, life, and the *chavurah*, went on, and the only casualty was the couple whose better half had taken such offense at the Gomeses' first Tupperware appearance. The woman and her husband refused to be part of a group that tolerated such small-mindedness, and eventually joined a more homogeneous *chavurah*. Ovadyah was particularly puzzled by the fact that the insulted woman was, like him, a "Jew by choice." Why couldn't she understand? It bothered him for a long time.

The *chavurah* turned out to be a mixed bag. There were genuinely good times, such as the group's sukkah party and Purim play, and some of the discussions and speakers were very interesting and worthwhile, the Gomeses thought. But they noticed that the best meetings revolved around political or social issues. The more religious the subject, the more disjointed the gathering, and the less satisfying.

Once, the *chavurah* dedicated an entire season of meetings to studying Genesis. Things did not go well at all.

"'In the beginning, God created the heavens and the earth,'" the leader of the first session began.

"Now what was He doing before that point?"

"You're really asking a question about the nature of time," replied another gentleman in

60

attendance, a professor, "whether there can ever have really been a `beginning.'"

"And you're both taking very literally what is, after all, only a human document recording the musings of a scientifically unsophisticated mind," the resident cynic noted.

"Well, one can approach the Bible in different ways," Ovadyah submitted, "and the traditional way is to consider it of Divine origin."

"Or Divinely inspired," the professor corrected, "like Franklin always says." Eager to remind people how Rabbi Shoman and he had been friends as boys, he liked to use the rabbi's first name. "Well, what's *that* supposed to mean?" Ariella asked.

"Just what I said," the cynic came in on cue. "A person, or people, wrote it, so take it with quite a few grains of salt."

"I think we should take it as God's word," Ovadyah tried again, "and try to brainstorm what He might have meant for us to learn from the words `in the beginning.'"

There was a moment of silence and then, to Ovadyah and Ariella's surprise, the group actually took the suggestion. Discussion ensued about the wording of the first verse, its grammar, structure and intent. However, after a half-hour of lively and far-ranging opinions thrown around the living room, a disturbed look fell over Ovadyah's face.

"I was just thinking — you know, we're trying to interpret the word of God but we're working with an English translation of the original language. Isn't that a problem?"

"Well, what would you suggest?" the professor asked. "*I* certainly don't know enough Hebrew to analyze the document in question. Do *you*?"

The barely camouflaged snideness in the professor's question flew right past Ovadyah. He was thinking too hard about the problem itself, the futility of serious Bible study in translation.

"Maybe we need to start learning Hebrew, then," he replied, "or at least approach the text using one of the traditional Jewish commentaries. Many of their authors, as I understand it, were outstanding Hebrew grammarians, and their commentaries are available in English."

"We would certainly benefit from their knowledge of the original language," Ariella concurred. "Oh please!" protested the cynic. "Here we are, intelligent, modern adults perfectly capable of taking our own approach to an ancient text, and you are suggesting that we resurrect some medieval religious scholar to guide us at every step! I can't believe this is happening."

"I second the motion to continue as we were. It was really a very stimulating discussion we were having."

"I third it," the host said with a smile. "Rather than lock ourselves into the approaches of the past, I think what we want to do is update that past and create our own commentaries."

"Without even studying the text in its original language," Ariella added with thunderously quiet sarcasm.

After a moment of awkward silence, someone said, "Well, we'll do the best we can."

"After all," another *chavurah* member spoke up for the first time, "it's the intellectual stimulation that really counts. That's what we want to access."

Ovadyah and Ariella stayed silent for the rest of the far-flung discussion. It seemed to them that each participant was just speaking his or her own mind, not really caring about the object of their "study." It was as if the Bible were just a vehicle for their own preconceived notions.

After another half-hour or so, when people began to repeat themselves, the discussion dissolved and everyone, looking unusually tired, bid everyone else goodbye.

The next day, the hosts for the following week's meeting arranged for a speaker to discuss the topic of Yiddish theater.

CHAPTER 10

Forbidden Fruit

The chavurah became less a focus of Ovadyah and Ariella's lives as time went on so they turned to the adult education program at Beth Am — which Ovadyah directed — for intellectual and religious nourishment.

There were actually two programs for continuing Jewish education, as it was called, at the synagogue. One was designed for Beth Am's steadily increasing number of converts. The program was more support group than pedagogical venture, a sort of "Goyim Anonymous," but it was well attended and much enjoyed by the participants. More than a dozen recent converts joined several potential ones each week to voice their concerns and fears about interacting with the Jewish-born congregants around them, usually starting with their spouses. Sometimes they just talked among themselves, other times someone would speak on a topic germane to joining the Jewish community. At each meeting, a mental health professional was on hand to monitor the psychological states of those present and to offer counseling in case the discussion became too emotionally strenuous for anyone. That service was thankfully never needed, but Rabbi Shoman felt better having the professional there just in case.

Ovadyah attended these sessions for "Jews by choice" — whom he and Ariella had jokingly dubbed "the convertibles" — religiously, though he himself would have prescribed more organized study and less dissection of each convert's culture shock. Having never anguished much over treeless Decembers or eggless Aprils, he had difficulty relating to those who did. He was troubled by what he saw as whining; there was just too much to *learn*.

The other educational program was the mainstream venture, and it truly intrigued Ovadyah and Ariella.

Rabbi Shoman gave one course, usually a suitably scholarly offering like "Christological Influences on Second-Century Pharisaic Judaism." Many attended the rabbi's courses, and all were impressed with the titles.

Rabbi Allen participated as well, sharing his expertise in education by teaching parents how to become part of their children's Jewish school experience. He particularly liked to show how easy and entertaining it was to "create a midrash," as he called it, to retell a Biblical story and invent new twists to the tale, rendering it "updated" and improved. The Talmudic rabbis, he would always point out, did much the same thing under the guise of transmitting ancient oral tradition. Why, then, he would ask in his introductory class, shouldn't we do the same today, without the guise?

Another rabbi connected to Beth Am taught Israeli dance, always a big draw. And a liturgy class was given by Mr. Finch, the unofficial rabbi of the "upstairs minyan."

The "upstairs minyan" was a traditional group who preferred daily rather than weekly services, and who felt more comfortable in the second-floor study than in the cavernous main sanctuary. Its members' memories of their fathers and grandfathers influenced the type of services they conducted, and Mr. Finch, a Holocaust survivor who wanted to provide some tradition for those who wanted it, eventually found himself acting as director of the group. While Beth Am was officially egalitarian, meaning that no ritual or role was gender-specific, the "upstairs minyan" allowed only men to lead the services and be called to the Torah. Mr. Finch had insisted on that point, conceding only that men and women be allowed to sit together, something no Orthodox congregation sanctioned. The synagogue rabbis rarely attended daily services upstairs, but they appreciated being able to direct more traditional congregants — those wanting to attend services on the anniversary of a relative's death, for instance, or during their year of mourning for a close relative — to the second-floor study.

As the director of the "upstairs minyan," Mr. Finch received a modest salary and was duly honored by the congregation every few years with a small gift thanking him for his efforts. Rabbi Shoman had mixed feelings about the man, however, especially when several congregants began to view him as some sort of religious authority. Though Mr. Finch was certainly familiar with the services and rituals, he had no rabbinic training, and Rabbi Shoman made sure his congregants knew it. The lack of equality for women at the daily services also ate at the rabbi's soul, but he felt that as long as Finch forwarded all important questions to the real rabbis, he served a purpose.

In addition to the classes offered by Beth Am personnel, Ovadyah had helped arrange for a teacher from Hope Heights Hebrew Day School, the Orthodox institution Ariella had once visited on business, to teach a course on the Ten Commandments.

When Rabbi Shoman heard of the innovation, he was somewhat perturbed. The Orthodox, he felt, were always looking to slander the more modern Jewish movements. It seemed as if every time some Orthodox person came in contact with members of Beth Am, he would make them uncomfortable, challenging the very premises of Conservative Judaism. Rabbi Shoman certainly disliked the idea of actually granting the Orthodox a platform from which to speak to his congregants. But the flyers had already gone out by the time he realized who "Rabbi Sinsky" was, so he decided to let it go. The Ten Commandments, he reassured himself with a sigh, were innocuous enough.

What he did catch in time, though, was the reading list Ovadyah had prepared for several of the courses. The very evening after Rabbi Shoman received it, Ovadyah stood summoned before him.

"Abel, er, Ovadyah," he began with a benevolent smile, "I'm having a few problems with one or two things on the syllabus here."

"Problems?" Ovadyah asked in all earnestness.

"Well, for instance, take the book *A Guide for the Jewish Homemaker* by Rose Blumenthal. First of all, do you know that the author's husband is an Orthodox rabbi?"

Ovadyah did, admitted as much, and then squinted in uncertainty as to the fact's import.

"Well," the rabbi continued, a bit of impatience poking its way through his benevolence, "we certainly don't want to discourage anyone from identifying with Judaism, do we?"

"No," Ovadyah had to agree.

"So asking them to read a book that is bound to reflect a position diametrical to ours just isn't wise. After all, more than a few potential converts attend our continuing education program. What will they think?"

"But the book had nothing objectionable in it," Ovadyah protested. "I've read it cover to cover. The author is liberal-minded, reasonable and very open to all Jews."

"Mr. Gomes," the rabbi's tone changed markedly, his benevolence burned off like morning fog, "you don't seem to understand. Blumenthal's apparent liberalness makes her all the more dangerous to sensitive Conservative Jews. Do you really want to tell our congregants and potential congregants that they have to, to...I don't know, tear toilet paper before Shabbat or some ridiculous notion like that? I mean, you've read the book. It reduces Judaism to countless, meaningless prohibitions and rules. I'm afraid you're being naive if you don't see that the book may well dissuade people from pursuing the larger social vision of Judaism."

Ovadyah hadn't thought of that, and now that it had been brought to his attention, he wasn't sure he agreed. But the rabbi was the rabbi so the book was scratched from the list, as were several others, for similar reasons.

Ovadyah had been taken aback by the rabbi's hostility toward Orthodoxy, though he had encountered it before at Beth Am. It was projected quite regularly from the pulpit on Friday nights, when one or another of the rabbis would address the subject of "right-wing extremism." Whenever the Israeli government periodically dredged up the possibility of amending that country's "Law of Return" to define Jews according to the guidelines of codified Jewish law, the rabbis at Beth Am would take thundering offense. One of them once banged his fist dramatically on the podium and compared these Orthodox proposals to the Nuremberg Laws. Ovadyah retained a particularly vivid memory of how the Orthodox were often accused of considering non-Orthodox Jews to be gentiles. He wondered if that were really true but couldn't imagine the rabbis making up such a thing.

And then there was the conversation Ovadyah and Ariella had overheard on Simchat Torah. Following tradition, Rabbi Shoman had held a Torah scroll and led a procession of congregants around the sanctuary. When the sedate ceremony was over, Ovadyah and Ariella were mingling in the adjoining social hall when someone in the group suddenly said, "Hey, who wants to go to HHH?" referring to Hope Heights Hebrew Day School. "I hear it's really lively there — singing and dancing, the works! And it goes on until the wee hours!"

Another voice concurred, "You're not kidding. I went there last year on a lark and it really was an experience."

But just as Ovadyah and Ariella were becoming intrigued, several others voiced their outrage at the suggestion.

"You don't want to go *there*," one said derisively, "if you know what's good for you. They don't think anyone's Jewish but their own. Those fanatics would just as soon spit on you as look at you."

The first speakers countered that they had felt very welcome at HHH the previous year, but the others just smiled condescendingly and shook their heads.

Ovadyah wanted to go and see for himself but, realizing his appearance would likely give him away as a convert, and knowing that the Orthodox certainly didn't recognize any conversions but their own, he and Ariella just went home.

Home was also precisely where Ovadyah went after his discussion with Rabbi Shoman. As always, he shared his thoughts with Ariella.

"Well," she said after a moment's thought, "you know those folks who pooh-poohed the idea of visiting HHH on Simchat Torah were mostly parents of kids at the Finkelstein School. They just had a bone to pick with the Orthodox school. It's their competition, after all."

"But it's more than that," Ovadyah reflected. "The Finkelstein School was founded by parents who'd soured on the Orthodox school. Its very raison d'être is the rejection of Hope Heights Hebrew Day School. Any suggestion that HHH has something to offer probably stings those folks something mean."

Ariella nodded in agreement.

"But you know what really struck me as the most negative of all the anti-Orthodox speeches over the past few months?"

"The time Meir Kahane came to town and Rabbi Shoman called him a Hitler?"

"No. When that rabbi who teaches Israeli dancing gave the sermon about that incident in Poland when that Orthodox man wouldn't let the woman rabbi conduct services in some ancient synagogue."

"You're not sounding like your feminist self," Ovadyah noted.

"But it had nothing to do with feminism, dear. The guy just felt that any departure from tradition would have been an affront to the memories of the pious Orthodox rabbis who had built and used that synagogue, and to the few Jews left in Cracow. I mean, you didn't have to agree with the guy's belief system to understand his feelings."

"But he tore her tallit off!" Ovadyah reminded his wife, referring to the widely reported description of the bearded, Orthodox man violently ripping the rabbi's prayer shawl from her shoulders.

"Don't you remember? The man vehemently denied ever doing that. And even if he did overreact, I still don't think it was right for the rabbi to attack him so viciously, to portray the guy as such a monster, when all he was doing was protecting the past."

"Did it really bother you so much then?" Ovadyah asked with some surprise.

"Yeah, it did," Ariella said pensively. "Especially since it was Rosh HaShanah, when the key theme is repentance and goodwill among Jews. I just thought it was no time to attack a fellow Jew just for having different values."

Ovadyah remembered now and had to agree that the sermon had indeed increased the hostility toward the Orthodox. The dancing rabbi, he felt, would have done better to have danced around the whole business.

CHAPTER 11

Unjust Deserts

E xcellent," Ovadyah pronounced as he patted his mouth with his napkin.

"Indeed," Ariella agreed, proud to have been the impetus for their visiting the restaurant.

Though she enjoyed cooking, her job sent her home each evening exhausted. And since their adoption of the Jewish dietary laws, she and Ovadyah, once avid restaurant-goers, had become largely homebound. So the opportunity to eat out was a special treat.

The Chowder Pot, they knew, was not technically a kosher restaurant like those they'd heard of in New York or Boston, which boasted an exclusively observant clientele and ongoing, official Orthodox rabbinical supervision. But the place was clean and classy — despite its name — and, most important, Rabbi Shoman had deemed it permissible to eat there.

Only the previous week, the rabbi had so informed his congregants. Although the restaurant served shellfish, he had looked into the situation and spoken to the management, and he was satisfied that the trout, scrod, salmon and vegetable side dishes were acceptable — as well as delectable, he'd added with a gourmet's knowing smile. "Each dish is prepared separately," he'd explained, "and I've seen to it that the chefs use separate pots and pans for the kosher fish."

Ariella was overjoyed that some respite from her daily kitchen chores was finally available. And now, seated at a quiet table in the back of the restaurant, sampling the fried scrod before her, she found that the rabbi's taste had proved trustworthy.

"Of course, it's not as good as your cooking, dear," Ovadyah made sure to add between forkfuls.

Ariella registered a wry half-smile.

"You know, we might be allowed to eat here," she reminded her husband, "but I don't recall the rabbi permitting anyone to lie!"

"You know," Ovadyah reflected, "it's really amazing that the rabbi managed to see things through to kasher this place."

"I was thinking the same thing myself," Ariella mused. "I mean, not only did he have to explain the whole business to the staff and convince them it was worthwhile to cater to kosher-keepers, but he had to boil up all those dishes and forks and knives and stuff." Ariella hesitated. "I guess he did, didn't he?"

"I'm sure he kept to the highest standards," Ovadyah reassured his wife, realizing that she was recalling Rabbi Allen's disturbingly offhanded approach to Jewish law when he'd visited their kitchen months earlier.

"Rabbi Allen is more into education than practical rabbinics," he continued. "When he came to our house that day and told us our pots and pans didn't need koshering, I'm sure he just wasn't thinking clearly. But Rabbi Shoman, well, he's the head honcho. I'm sure he knew just what he was doing."

"I suppose so.... I wonder how he got the kitchen staff to agree to keep separate utensils and areas for the kosher food."

"I'll bet it wasn't easy."

Ovadyah's eyes suddenly lit up.

"Hey! Let's go check out the kitchen. It'll be interesting to see how things were set up."

Ariella was hesitant. Waiters were constantly exploding through the swinging doors separating patrons from provender, making the inner sanctum of the restaurant seem decidedly off-limits to casual visits.

But Ovadyah was determined. His curiosity was piqued, and long ago he had learned that going where one didn't belong required only the banishment of self-consciousness. If he were to just walk in as if he owned the place, he knew no one would suspect that he didn't.

"I'll just be a couple of minutes," he said as he rose from his seat.

Ariella considered stopping him, but she reminded herself that once he was intent on seeing something through, he could not be daunted. That explained a lot about him, she mused with a smile after he had disappeared through the swinging doors, like how he had come to where he was in life. And how he had brought her along.

Having left his wife to her thoughts, Ovadyah strode purposefully through the restaurant's large kitchen.

"And where exactly are the kosher fish dishes prepared?" he abruptly asked a chef who seemed to have an air of authority about him.

"And who are you?" came the cold reply.

Ovadyah quickly weighed several possible responses. He decided on, "Who do you *think* I am?" It was a good choice. Caught off guard, the cook sputtered and eventually admitted he had no idea.

"Well, you know Rabbi Shoman, don't you?"

The name smelled familiar to the chef, like some bouillabaisse from long ago. Suddenly it dawned on him that the well-dressed man who had visited the kitchen accompanied by the owner of the establishment several weeks earlier had been introduced as "Rabid Showman," or so he had thought at the time. It had struck him as an odd name. Then he remembered the caution the owner had relayed in the gentleman's presence that day about dietary restrictions some people had. He had understood it as some sort of allergy to shellfish and had agreed to make sure that anyone requesting a shellfish-free entrée received one. So the guy had been a rabbi, the cook now realized. Funny, he hadn't looked like one.

"Why, yes, of course I know Rabbi Shoman," the grand chef told Ovadyah with more than a hint of insult at the insinuation that he might not. Then, stopping to eyeball the even less rabbinical-looking man he was talking to — for goodness sake, he thought, he's not even the right color for a rabbi — he asked, "You are here for the rabbi?"

Ovadyah didn't miss a beat. Ignoring the question entirely, he smiled curtly and said, "Now can we get to the business at hand?"

The chef, somewhat confused but interested only in ridding his kitchen of this nuisance, led him to where the salmon and trout were prepared and cooked. Once he began the tour, however, pride in his operation overtook him and he eagerly described what each junior cook was doing.

"And here, fillet of trout is being readied for broiling. My cook is preparing the scallions, shallots, parsley, chives and tarragon to be sautéed first — *Leo, get some oil over here!* — I'm sorry, pardon me for shouting."

"Quite all right," Ovadyah said magnanimously as he watched an older, balding man with a soiled apron carry a deep pan of hot oil to where they stood. He carefully poured some oil into the skillet the younger cook was tending.

"Why is the oil preheated?" Ovadyah asked out of curiosity.

"Well, it does have to reach a certain temperature before the scallions and shallots are added, but the oil isn't `preheated,' it's `pre-*used*.' We use it several times for different dishes. Very little actually enters the foods but delicate aromas are absorbed by the remainder, which makes it — "

"What?"

"Pardon?"

"Forgive me," Ovadyah caught himself, reassuming his calm, "in charge" voice. "What I meant was, what sort of dishes is the oil usually taken from?"

"Oh, whatever's handy."

"I see. And could you tell where, say, this oil before us originated?"

The chef deftly snapped up a basting brush from the counter and ran it across the sizzling oil in the skillet. After waving the sample in the air to cool it, he touched his finger to the brush and then to his tongue.

"Shrimp!" he pronounced with no small satisfaction.

"Shrimp?" Ovadyah echoed without the triumphant tone.

"Shrimp," confirmed the chef with finality. "The subtle aroma is unmistakable and will add much to the vegetables, allowing them to complement the trout beautifully. We might, of course, re-use the oil yet again for, say, frying potatoes…"

Ovadyah was mortified. Having heard quite enough, he offered a hasty thanks to the puzzled chef, who was just beginning to enjoy speaking with his interested and most attentive visitor.

As Ovadyah reentered the dining area and approached his table, Ariella greeted him.

"So the inspector general returns."

Then she saw the look on her husband's face and knew something was amiss.

"What's wrong?" she asked.

"I can't believe it," he said quietly, his agitation showing. "They re-use the same oil for everything they cook."

The implications for the *kashrut* of anything at the restaurant were obvious.

A frown spread across Ariella's face.

"I better call Rabbi Shoman and let him know right away!" Ovadyah said suddenly, darting toward the phones at the far end of the room.

Ariella was left once more to her thoughts — and to a sad, sinking feeling. After all their efforts to keep kosher, here they had blown their "diet" entirely, albeit inadvertently. And all because of some mixup on the part of the kitchen staff. About to blame herself for having been so anxious to eat out, she saw Ovadyah returning to the table. He looked at her strangely, saying nothing. "Did you get through to the rabbi?"

"Not exactly. Only Beverly was in the office."

A Judaic studies teacher at the Finkelstein School, Beverly was widely respected for her innovative and creative educational methods."

"And?"

Ovadyah hesitated and his puzzled look intensified, garnished<%0> with pain. Finally, he answered.

"I told her what I had seen."

"So what did she say?"

"Well, first she tried to convince me that I had probably made some mistake. But when I insisted that I knew what I saw, all she said was, `So who told you to go snooping around in the kitchen?'"

Ovadyah's expression spread to Ariella's face.

They left their desserts untouched.

CHAPTER 12

Continuing Education

Dina Rosen felt bad for the two little girls. The birthday party had ended twenty minutes earlier and there she stood, her own daughter in tow, ready to go home. But she couldn't bring herself to abandon the pair of six-year-olds still waiting for their ride. The birthday girl's parents were busy cleaning up so Dina walked over to the two kids sitting quietly on the steps in front of the house. She hadn't really noticed their faces before; they had just been two frail bundles huddled together in their aloneness. Now, though, she saw that they were clearly twins, and she was struck by their unusual beauty. They smiled shy, delicate smiles as she approached them, and their tan skin seemed somehow radiant. They looked like Sephardim, Oriental Jews, Dina thought to herself.

"Hi, girls!" she began cheerily. "What are your names?"

Each bundle unfolded a bit and two pairs of eyes glanced at their inquisitor's face and then at her feet.

"Ruth."

"Daphna."

Their sweet, quiet voices, barely whispers, were even more endearing.

"Well, this is Tanya," she said, pointing to her own little girl, "as I guess you already know, and I'm Mrs. Rosen. Are you waiting for someone to pick you up?"

"Our father's coming soon," one of the twins — Dina had already forgotten who was who — answered with calm confidence.

"Should I wait with you?" she asked, trying hard to sound earnest.

The twins' simultaneous smiles said, "Yes."

Only a moment later, a car pulled up, a swarthy, well-dressed m<%0>an its only occupant.

Dina watched as the man emerged and approached her and her charges. He seemed vaguely African at first, but when he got closer, Dina guessed he might have South American or West Indian roots. She wished him a good afternoon but failed to make the connection until the twins were firmly in his embrace.

"Oh! You're Ruth and Daphna's father!" she found herself exclaiming, slightly embarrassed at her own surprise. "I'm Dina Rosen. I was just keeping them company until you came."

"Why, that was so nice of you," Ovadyah replied. "I was delayed getting here and I'm so glad they had someone nice to wait with. I'm Ovadyah Gomes."

He extended his hand but the pleasant young woman didn't take it.

"I'm sorry, I'm Orthodox," Dina explained while his hand hovered lonely in the air.

Ovadyah didn't know what to make of *that*. What did one have to do with the other? And *she* was *Orthodox*? She seemed perfectly normal to him — other than her strange aversion to hands. An attractive, polite, friendly Orthodox person? Something wasn't clicking.

"Oh," he said, not knowing what else might possibly be appropriate.

"Please don't be offended," Dina went on. "It's nothing personal. It's just that Orthodox Jews try to avoid physical contact between men and women who aren't married to each other. It's really not as crazy as it sounds, just a bit unusual in today's society. But anyway, it's a pleasure to meet you, Mr. Gomes."

As she said his name, she realized she had heard it before. Suddenly, it dawned on her that her own husband had mentioned it recently.

"Are you by any chance on the Jewish Federation's Israel Task Force?" she asked Ovadyah.

"Why, yes, as a matter of fact, I am," he admitted. It was one of several committees and organizations for which he had volunteered since his conversion.

"Well, then I think you've met my husband," she said. "Ron? He's on it, too, and I think he mentioned your name the other night."

"Why, of course," Ovadyah acknowledged. "The name Rosen bounced right off me. It's a special pleasure to meet his better half."

"Well, his other half, anyway," Dina interjected.

"That's not what he told me," Ovadyah demurred.

74

He remembered Ron Rosen well as the young man who had immediately befriended him at the first meeting of the task force. They had spoken for only a few minutes that night, yet Ron had managed to invite Ovadyah and his family to spend Shabbat at his home. That had really impressed him. He had just met the guy and was already invited to his house for a weekend!

Dina interrupted Ovadyah's memories with a question that made him chuckle.

"Why don't you and your family come and spend a Shabbat with us sometime?" she asked. Dina wondered at Ovadyah's little laugh.

"That would be very nice, I'm sure," he replied. "But maybe we could just come for a meal instead."

"Do you live in the neighborhood?" Dina asked with a hint of hesitation.

Ovadyah knew what the lady was getting at. She didn't want to cause him to drive on Shabbat. He owned up to the facts:

"I'm afraid we don't."

"So come Friday afternoon and stay until Saturday night!" Dina announced enthusiastically. "We'd really love to have you, all of you." She then turned to the girls and asked them, "Would you guys like to spend Shabbat with us?"

They nodded a shy but unmistakable "yes."

"Well that does it!" Dina told Ovadyah. "You wouldn't deny your lovely daughters' request, would you?"

"I wouldn't *dare*," Ovadyah conceded with mock fear of the consequences. Then, his tone resolute, he added, "I'll certainly talk to my wife about it, and I do thank you for the invitation."
"You're very welcome — and I guarantee we'll make you feel welcome if you take us up on our offer!" Dina took a piece of paper and a pen from her purse, jotted down her phone number and handed it to Ovadyah. "It was really nice meeting you, Mr. Gomes. Bye, girls!"

The twins waved and their father opened the car door for them.

After dinner that evening, as the girls played in the living room, Ovadyah told Ariella about meeting Dina Rosen — including her reluctance to shake his hand — and about her invitation. The previous week, he had told her about meeting Ron and *his* offer to have them for Shabbat. Her reaction then had been lukewarm. Now it was downright chilly.

"Are they normal?" she asked bluntly.

"Ariella dear, they are two of the nicest people you'd ever want to meet," Ovadyah assured her. "So why are they inviting three people they hardly know — and one they don't at all — to spend a weekend with them?"

"*Chessed?*" he suggested, using the Hebrew word that encompasses the whole gamut of acts of goodwill toward others.

Ariella smiled, disarmed.

"Well, that's very admirable on their part," she said, "but Ovadyah, do you really want to spend twenty-odd hours with these people? We could be bored silly."

"I guess that could happen...but maybe we'll like them and enjoy the visit. What's a day anyway? And whatever happened to your spirit of adventure?"

"All right," she gave in, as she'd known all along she would; she had just felt someone should supply some counterpoint. "But if Shabbat turns out to be a bummer, we do something exciting on Sunday."

"Deal," Ovadyah agreed, extending his hand.

"Sorry," Ariella said with exaggerated insult, "I don't shake hands with men."

The Rosens were overjoyed to have their invitation accepted, even if it would be two weeks before the Gomes family could come for Shabbat. The coming week, a special program was scheduled at Beth Am and Ovadyah and Ariella didn't want to miss it.

The "Visiting Scholars Program" was part of the synagogue's "Educational Shabbaton" series. That Shabbat, a dean of the "CTC," the Conservative Theological College, was to conduct various seminars for the congregants in attendance.

The Conservative Theological College was the premier rabbinical seminary of the Conservative movement, and Rabbi Isaiah Shintov, one of its brightest stars. Born in Eastern Europe and educated there in a famous yeshivah, he had arrived in the United States just prior to the Second World War and joined the staff of the CTC shortly thereafter, establishing himself as both a legal scholar and one of the foremost proponents of Conservative Judaism.

Rabbi Shintov lived up to the latter reputation when he spoke from the pulpit at Beth Am on Friday night. During an "Ask the Rabbi" question-and-answer session, one congregant asked him to comment on the Conservative movement's relationship to ancient Jewish tradition. With a slight Slavic accent but perfect grammar, he proceeded to illustrate that Jewish law had not remained static but had *developed* over the Talmudic era, contending that "adapting to the times" had always been the rabbis' prime concern, "just as it is," he shouted like a klieg-lit candidate, "the very hallmark of the modern Jewish path, Conservative Judaism."

The applause that followed encouraged him to press the issue further and challenge his audience to demonstrate the courage of its convictions.

"The authentic heir to the Talmudic tradition is unquestionably the Conservative movement," he intoned with academic authority. "Haven't you all, by the very fact of your worship here, reached the same conclusion?"

As it happened, that was hardly the case. Most members of Beth Am had precious little idea of what the Conservative movement stood for, and less still of what the Talmud was. They had joined the synagogue simply because it offered them a comfortable religious environment, undemanding yet dignified. Rabbi Shintov himself knew as much from his extensive travels around the country, but he always spoke as if every Conservative Jew had become one only after careful research and soul-searching.

"So I'd like to ask you all a question," he continued slowly, "and have you answer with a show of hands."

The audience, several hundred people, fidgeted as one.

"How many of you," he articulated dramatically, "support Orthodox institutions?" He pronounced the word "Orthodox" as if it were a disease.

After a moment, a few hands slowly went up, and then a good many more.

"I have only one question of you," he announced, confident that the unraised hands belonged to cowardly folk who simply would not admit their support. (Almost every Conservative Jew, he knew, gave to one or another Orthodox charity.) After pausing for effect, he leaned into the microphone and thundered, "*Why?!*"

Pausing again, the speaker looked around. All hands had retreated to the security of their owners' laps. He continued, now more quietly, to speak.

"Don't you realize that if we are right, they are *wrong*? That they hate us passionately — regardless of what they claim — and would be dancing in the streets tomorrow if the Conservative movement disappeared tonight? That, to them, we are something less than full *Jews*?" Another pause. "And you can still write them *checks*?!"

Ariella turned to her husband and whispered, "A little shrill, don't you think?" Dozens of other congregants were conveying similar sentiments to their spouses or to themselves.

Ovadyah agreed wholeheartedly. While he understood that the Orthodox were backward and unappealing, he saw no need to badmouth or harm them. Just because some Jews didn't realize the importance of keeping up with the times didn't make them the *enemy*, for goodness sake. To Ariella, he just nodded and said quietly, "What's he so afraid of? The Orthodox won't last."
After services, Ovadyah and Ariella stood in line waiting to greet the guest scholar.

"Do you think he's right about the Orthodox being such monsters?" Ariella asked her husband.
 "Well, I'll tell you one thing," he replied. "The Rosens hardly seem monstrous. They don't seem capable of hate. Should we ask the rabbi to explain what he meant more clearly?"

"I don't know, dear. This doesn't seem a good time for a long discussion with him." They had moved a good way down the line but many others were waiting behind them. "And I did want to ask him that question we had about *niddah*."

Earlier that week, Ariella and Ovadyah had come across a book on the laws of *niddah*, usually politely referred to as "family purity laws." Jewish law forbids sexual relations when a wife is menstruating, and, under certain conditions, until a week after her period has ended. Since early Talmudic times, the extra week's prohibition has been applied to all cases. The Gomeses knew all that, though when they had spoken to Rabbi Shoman, he had seemed surprised to hear about the "additional week" rule and had counseled the couple to ignore it. They sensed that the entire concept of *niddah* didn't sit well with him.

In any case, the book they had recently read not only mandated the extra week's separation, but delineated the law as requiring abstention not only from sexual relations but from all physical contact. They had never heard that before and wanted to know if it was just some outdated Orthodox stringency or if modern, mainstream Judaism retained that limitation. As a Talmudic scholar, they reasoned, Rabbi Shintov could give them an authoritative answer.

When they reached him, he seemed shorter than he had when he'd stood at the podium. The strength of his delivery had somehow enlarged him, Ariella thought. He was sixtyish and well-groomed, with curly, gray hair and a neat, salt-and-pepper beard. He smiled and shook hands with each of them.

Before they moved on, Ariella seized the opportunity and asked her question about *niddah*.

Rabbi Shintov seemed taken aback at first. Having received only pleasantries from the line so far, he hadn't expected a halachic query from any of the smiling faces filing by. It took him only an instant, though, to regain his mental footing, and Ariella saw a glimmer in his eye as he comprehended the question.

"My dear young lady, please trust me," he began. "Such customs are pointless in our times. To forbid a husband and wife even to touch one another two weeks out of each month is a bit extreme, wouldn't you say? I will say more than that. It is more destructive than helpful to their marriage. Rest assured that you needn't consider mere physical contact prohibited at any point."
Then, as if to emphasize the point and more, Rabbi Shintov put his hand on Ariella's neck and pulled her toward him, giving her a friendly little hug.

"In Judaism, my dear," he concluded, "as in life in general, those who try to maintain the attitudes of the past in the present only subvert the future."

He let Ariella go, slapped Ovadyah good-naturedly on the shoulder and wished them both, "Shabbat shalom," as the line behind them pushed them on.

CHAPTER 13

Unfinished Symphony

A delicious smell hit them squarely as soon as Ron opened the door for them. The aroma was strong but complex; Ovadyah and Ariella were surprised to find themselves so suddenly hungry.

"Hi, folks!" Ron greeted his guests. "We're so happy you made it."

Dina, wearing an apron and a kerchief, called out from the kitchen, "Hi, everybody! Excuse me for letting Ron show you your rooms. I'm running a little late, as usual." The ladle in her hand and the perspiration on her face broadcast her point.

"Please," Ariella insisted, "just stay where you are. And let me give you a hand as soon as we get settled."

"Thanks so much," Dina smiled. "I'm really mostly done here in the kitchen, but I'll let you set the table if you don't mind."

"I'll be right there," Ariella replied. Then she turned to Ron. "Lead on!" she said.

Upstairs, Ron showed Ovadyah and Ariella to a small but pleasant room. He then took the twins to his own daughter's bedroom. After clothes were hung up, the kids began to play together and the parents headed back downstairs.

Ron invited his guests to relax a bit, indicating the couch, but Ariella protested, "Uh-uh, I've got a date in the kitchen," and went to join Dina. Ovadyah sat down, expecting a bit of conversation with his host, but Ron immediately excused himself, disappeared for a moment, and then rematerialized with a vacuum cleaner, which he quickly plugged in, turned on and deftly wielded across the floor.

Ovadyah marveled at all that was happening at once in the oddly animated home. As Ron passed to and fro before him, carefully cleaning the carpet, Ovadyah saw Ariella and Dina gliding back and forth from the kitchen to the dining area, where silver candlesticks and cutlery sparkled atop an immaculate, white tablecloth. Their laughter and conversation wafted over on a cloud of scrumptious steam from the pots on the stove. The noise of the vacuum cleaner muffled the words but not their mood: rushed, spirited, happy, alive. The high-pitched sounds of the children playing trickled down from upstairs and everything — sounds, sights and smells — enveloped Ovadyah like some multisensory symphony. He wanted a part in the orchestra, too.

"What can I do?" he shouted to Ron over the din of the vacuum.

Ron shut off the machine and said, "Well, there are some folding chairs upstairs in the second room on the right. We're having some other guests for dinner tonight and we'll need — let's see — three more chairs down here. Would you mind?"

"Not at all," Ovadyah said, meaning it, and soon the clatter of too many chairs being carried at once brought some percussion to the concert. A few moments later, the men moved some furniture from the living room to make room for the folding table they had brought up from the basement.

"The lights!" Dina called from the kitchen. "Ron, don't forget the lights!"

"Oh thanks!" Ron called back, adding to himself, "I almost did."

Ovadyah watched as his host set timers in the living room and dining room and then put the light on in the bathroom and taped the switch.

"Sometimes Tanya forgets it's Shabbat and turns the light off," Ron explained.

Ovadyah understood the problem. If that happened, they wouldn't be permitted to turn the lights on again.

"And the Sabbath is supposed to be honored with light," he offered, recalling the fact from his reading.

"That's right," Ron confirmed, "though in the case of the bathroom, I think it's more of a matter of urgency than honor!"

"I suppose so," Ovadyah admitted with a laugh.

"The Talmud also says that a bright house is a peaceful house, and the Sabbath is a time of peace," Ron noted.

In that spirit, he proceeded to place rounded, glass inserts into the silver candlesticks, carefully filled them with olive oil and inserted floating wicks in each now-golden orb. Ovadyah marveled at the beautiful gold-and-silver results, which now awaited only the woman of the house to consummate their glory by lighting the wicks and ushering in the Sabbath with their flames.

Ron excused himself to shower for Shabbat and Ovadyah, after checking on the kids, returned to the living room, where the audio-visual symphony had concluded but the olfactory one continued, as it would throughout the night. He joined Ariella on the couch.

"Wow, it was like a whirlwind in here before," she greeted him.

"Tell me about it," her husband agreed. "I sort of got sucked up into it, too!"

"Well, good for you," Ariella said, and then she lapsed into quiet thought for a moment before speaking again. "But it was *nice*, wasn't it?"

"I know what you mean." Ovadyah's quick response clearly indicated that he had been thinking the same thought. "It really was. And it's become so peaceful now." He looked at his watch. "I can't believe it — it's almost time for services."

As if on cue, Ron came hurtling down the stairs, tying his necktie as he bounced, his hair still damp and his clean, white shirt untucked.

"Five-minute warning!" he told his guests, not missing a beat in his quest for his shoes.

Ovadyah suddenly couldn't remember where he had put his own jacket and began looking around frantically.

Dina then descended the stairs, somewhat less hurriedly than her husband. She, too, was freshly showered, and the towel on her head matched the elegant, colorful robe she wore.

"Aren't you going to services?" Ariella asked, realizing that five minutes would barely give Dina a chance to dry her hair.

"Oh, no, I don't go to shul very often. Very few women are there on Friday night anyway. And I've still got to light candles, feed the baby and make some last-minute preparations for the meal."

Ariella visualized all the couples seated together at Beth Am on Friday night and she frowned. Dina noticed.

"Please, Ariella," she assured her guest, "feel free to go to shul if you want to. I don't need any help here now, and I really do enjoy bringing in Shabbat at home more than attending services."
"If you don't mind," Ariella said, "I think I'll stay too." Then she addressed the men, who by then had found all their clothing. "C'mon, guys, you don't want to be late! I'm sticking around here with Dina. We'll see you later."

"You sure you don't want to come along, Ariella?" Ovadyah asked, feeling strange going to services without his wife.

"Of course, I'm sure. We wouldn't be sitting together anyway at an Orthodox synagogue. You boys run along now, don't talk to strangers, and stay out of trouble!" she added with a dollop of exaggerated condescension.

In an instant, the men were out the door. Ariella heard a car engine a moment later, its rumbling roar fading over several seconds to a distant buzz and finally to silence. Since there was still a half-hour to sunset, the Sabbath had not yet arrived so Ron could drive to services; his car would remain at the synagogue until the following night, after the Sabbath was over.

The children had gone into the backyard to play on the swings, and in the peaceful, almost soporific silence that settled over the house, the two women sat down together for the first time since they'd met.

For some reason, Ariella felt enough at ease with Dina to dispense with the vapid niceties usually exchanged during first conversations. She just let whatever thoughts suggested themselves flow from her mouth.

"Wouldn't you like to go to services, too?"

"Well," Dina began cautiously, not sure where to start, "first of all, there's the baby. You haven't met Ari yet, but he's due to wake up from his nap any minute. Not only is it too complicated to arrange his nursing schedule around services, but I'd have to get a sitter if I left the house. He doesn't walk yet, and we can't carry him to shul on Shabbat."

Ariella remembered that Orthodox Jews didn't "carry" on Shabbat. They wouldn't so much as step outside on the Sabbath while holding anything. She realized with a disturbing jolt that Dina was effectively housebound from Friday afternoon until Saturday night.

"Doesn't it give you cabin fever?" she asked.

"Not at all," Dina answered with a smile. "I'm not a shut-in. Whenever I want, Ron will babysit so I can get out for a while. Every Shabbat afternoon, I do just that to attend a *shiur*."

"A who?"

"A *shiur*. A *shiur* is a class, usually given by a local rabbi or his wife."

"Oh," Ariella said, unimpressed and taking no pains to hide it. "Do you ever get out *with* your husband?"

"Well, we sometimes take a walk after the kids are asleep on Friday night. We just go up and down the block so we can stay within sight of the house, but we enjoy the night air together anyway."

Ariella shook her head almost imperceptibly.

"It just seems so...so *oppressive*," she commented, instantaneously surprised at herself for lobbing such a judgment at Dina.

Dina took no offense.

"You mean my being at home so much?"

"Yes, that, but not only that," she said quietly.

For Ariella, one of the most important elements of worship at Beth Am was its treatment of men and women as equals, delegating honors and responsibilities in an egalitarian fashion. It was precisely with that attitude that the Conservative movement had so distanced itself from the unabashed sexism of the Orthodox.

"I mean," she continued, "Orthodoxy is so male-centered. Don't you feel left out?"

"No, not at all," Dina answered calmly. "I don't choose to look at it that way. Where you see a dried-up well, I see a shaft to a gold mine.

"At first, when Tanya was born, I think I did feel bad about having to give up going to services, but I've since come to really enjoy being at home. I look at it more like `holding the fort' than `being stuck at home.' After all, the whole Shabbat experience really revolves around the *home* — and I'm the one who's molding and directing that home."

"Come on, Dina. What about the services? Aren't they the real center stage of the Sabbath?"

"No, they're not. I guess a superficial observer might think they are, but the Sabbath meals are really what give the day its character and meaning, for both women *and* men."

Dina paused to gather her thoughts and then took a deep breath.

"But all that is really beside the point. Let me tell you something, Ariella. You won't understand it right now — I think I can imagine the baggage you're carrying — but if you keep an open mind and look at Judaism honestly, you'll see that having a role to play in life isn't a demeaning thing. It's no different from life itself. The people whose names never make the newspapers aren't any less important — and are often worlds more important — than the headliners and celebrities. Prominence doesn't equal worth. Men might seem more prominent in Judaism but they're not more important. As a matter of fact, I sometimes wonder if their prominence might even be intended to cushion the blow of lacking what women have. In a nutshell, Ron and I are complements of each other, not clones."

Ariella quashed a sudden and surprising feeling of empathy. She had always been an ardent feminist and a relentless assailant of male chauvinism wherever it reared its smirking face. Yet here, despite her knowledge that Orthodoxy was a hopelessly patriarchal cult, she found Dina's brand of "Orthodox feminism" strangely appealing. The lady was *embracing* femininity rather than measuring it by some male yardstick. Ariella caught herself, though, recalling how systems created by men had mistreated women throughout history.

"But you're *barred* from performing the rituals and responsibilities that men are allowed!" she practically sang out. "How can you possibly *defend* that?"

"To be honest, I stopped envying men their Torah readings and service leadings so long ago that I can't even imagine how a woman could be insulted by it all. Having and raising a child — forget the child! — just being the one to create the Jewish atmosphere at home is so much more meaningful, so much more *real* to me. It's hard to be resentful when I'm so happy with what I have."

Ariella was surprised at Dina's eloquence but she didn't allow herself to take her hostess's words as anything more than the rationalization of a sexist religion. She still felt just as sorry for Dina. "I suppose when you've grown up with a certain lifestyle," she mused aloud, "you learn how to come to terms with it."

Dina knit her brow.

"I didn't grow up Orthodox," she informed her guest. "It was a careful decision Ron and I made several years after we were married."

Ariella was stunned. People *became* Orthodox? She had assumed that Ron and Dina had inherited their way of life, that they represented a stage somewhere between their European parents' "old-time religion" and the inevitable liberalized Judaism that lay in the future. She thought *all* young Orthodox were the products of old Orthodox who had placed the albatross of their values firmly around their children's necks. While she wasn't entirely at a loss for words, she didn't know exactly how to react to what Dina had told her.

"You don't come from Orthodox roots?" she stammered.

"Well, maybe way back there somewhere," Dina explained. "After all, all our ancestors were Orthodox if you go back far enough. But my parents are Reform Jews and Ron's belong to a Conservative synagogue. Our grandparents weren't Orthodox, either. We chose Orthodoxy for ourselves."

"But why?" Ariella asked incredulously.

Dina laughed a friendly, heartfelt laugh. "That's not a question I can possibly answer before everyone comes home," she said. Then suddenly her eyes opened wide and she exclaimed, "Goodness! I've still got to wake and feed Ari! *Intermezzo*, Ariella! I'm sure we'll have more time to talk during dinner or later on tonight."

Dina squeezed Ariella's hand and excused herself, leaving her guest on the couch by herself. Ariella felt oddly refreshed, and relieved of her fear that the next twenty-four hours would be an endless, boring experience. She was actually looking forward to spending more time with Dina and her family. Savoring the perfectly quiet interlude before Ovadyah and Ron came home from synagogue, she tried to tune in to her feelings. Ariella was a little surprised, a little confused and more than a little intrigued.

CHAPTER 14

Turning Point

I can't believe how *blunt* I was," Dina told her husband quietly over the open refrigerator door. "Ron, I was talking to her like I had known her forever!"

The men had returned from the synagogue a half-hour earlier and when the other guests had arrived, Ron had led everyone in singing two songs before the Sabbath meal, one welcoming Shabbat, the other extolling the virtues of the "Woman of Valor." Then he had "made kiddush" — reciting the special blessings over wine that mark the start of the Sabbath meal. All the guests had now completed the ritual washing of hands required before eating bread; only the host and hostess had yet to wash. Dina wanted to take the horseradish out of the fridge first — and to talk to her husband alone in the kitchen. The refrigerator had been witness to many such quick, pre-Sabbath-meal tête-à-têtes.

Guests were the norm in the Rosens' home. Ron and Dina saw every Jew as a walking opportunity for *chessed*, as Ovadyah had rightly guessed weeks before. While Ron and Dina were always happy if any guest expressed interest in Orthodox observance — and they did their best to supply ideas and information to help any seeker along — they were no missionaries. They saw their encouragement of observance simply as part of their chessed, a service they were glad to provide to those who wanted it. Those who didn't received the same warm hospitality in the Rosen house, and with no less enthusiasm or goodwill.

"She had all her defenses up but I like her," Dina continued. "We had a good talk. I just hope my directness didn't turn her off."

"I wouldn't worry, honey," Ron assured her.

He knew his wife's style was nothing like what she had just described. She never forced issues, always accepted people for who they were, and empathized fully with every Jew who crossed their threshold, no matter where he or she stood on the wide Jewish spectrum. He doubted that she had really spoken harshly to Ariella, but if she had, he knew that it must have been because the guest had sought bluntness.

"She seems perfectly happy, not in the least upset," Ron reported after a glance into the dining room, "so I'd say she must have appreciated your honesty. You know, not everybody likes things sweet," he added, taking the jar of horseradish from Dina and dangling it pointedly before her.

Dina really hadn't planned on discussing Orthodoxy with Ariella at all over Shabbat. It had been Ariella who had brought up the subject and pushed it, she told herself. Still, her guest's intelligence and convictions had impressed Dina. Ariella seemed determined to get to the bottom of things rather than clinging stubbornly to positions that were anything less than totally honest. She knew they'd be talking more over Shabbat.

Ron interrupted her thoughts, reminding her that Ariella had another half and that he had just had his first experience in an Orthodox synagogue.

"Ovadyah seemed to really enjoy shul," he said as he filled a large, metal cup with water. "He was all eyes and ears, and he davened like a pro. He got some stares, of course, but he seemed unfazed by them. Everyone was certainly friendly to him, and I think he appreciated it. You know, he'd make a good Jew. I wonder if he'll get a proper conversion one day."

Ron realized that Ovadyah's conversion had most likely been authorized by a Conservative or Reform rabbi, which almost certainly meant that even if the rituals of *mikvah* and circumcision had been properly executed, the equally essential element of "acceptance of mitzvos" had been lacking, invalidating the procedure in the eyes of Jewish law. Only the Orthodox movement adhered to the age-old definition of "mitzvah" — an eternal, God-given commandment — so to the Orthodox, only Orthodox conversions were valid.

"*...al netilas yadayim,*" Ron completed the blessing on washing one's hands. Dina answered, "Amen." Then it was her turn to wash and say the blessing and Ron's to respond. They walked into the dining room to join their guests, who sat perfectly quiet. Ron had asked them to comply with Jewish tradition and refrain from talking between the ritual washing of hands and the partaking of bread. Now he was embarrassed at having tarried so long in the kitchen at the expense of his muzzled guests. Hurriedly, he sat down at the head of the table and said the blessing on the challah.

As Ron sliced the braided loaves and Dina passed pieces to her guests, Ovadyah looked around the table. He and Ariella were sitting to Ron's right, Dina to his left. In a highchair next to Dina sat her baby, Ari. Then came Tanya and, at the far end of the table, the other guests: a middle-aged couple and their teenage son. Noticing Ovadyah's glance, Ron introduced Ed and Susan Waldman and their son, Josh. Ron was a lawyer, he told Ovadyah and Ariella, as was Ed. They had met while representing different clients in the same case.

"Do you often invite rival lawyers to your home?" Ovadyah joked.

"When they let on they're Jewish, I do!" Ron replied, to everyone's laughter. "While we were hammering out an agreement between our clients, he told me I was *meshuga* when I tried to add a clause he didn't like. After his third Yiddish word, I knew he wasn't embarrassed by his Jewishness, so I made my move," Ron explained, as if describing the climax of a safari hunt.

"'Stalking the Wild Yid,' eh?" Ed quipped. "I've heard of ambulance-chasers, but not many lawyers would admit to Jew-chasing!"

"Well, I would!" Ron reiterated unabashedly. "We're all family, after all. If you discovered a cousin you didn't know you had, wouldn't you want to get to know him?"

No one could argue with that logic. Ovadyah knew that, despite his comic tone, Ron was serious. Here he and his wife were entertaining seven guests they hardly knew, whose only connection to their hosts was Jewishness. He'd never seen anything like that before.

"You guys are something else!" Ed said, shaking his head and echoing Ovadyah's thoughts. "You know, Ron, you're really too nice to be a lawyer."

"Hmm," Ron said with mock concern, "that might explain a few things..."

After the soup, Ron began to sing a Hebrew song. When nobody joined in, he cleared his throat exaggeratedly and announced the page in the bentchers, or songbooks, he had given everyone. Ovadyah, who had played the flute since his youth, quickly picked up the tune and joined in. The Waldmans excused themselves, explaining that they didn't read Hebrew, but Ron wouldn't hear of their remaining on the sidelines. Instead, he patiently taught them the words to the refrain and soon they, too, were singing along.

Two songs and several courses later, the mood had mellowed considerably. The younger children gone to play upstairs and a calm descended over the table. After Ron and the guests complimented Dina on the delicious, abundant food she'd served, everyone basked in the afterglow of the hearty meal. The Sabbath candles flickered gently and all was quiet for several moments. Ron's low humming was the only sound...until Ariella felt a sudden compulsion to disturb the peace.

"So I haven't heard about services tonight," she an>nounced to Ovadyah loudly enough to make his report the meal's conversation piece.

"They were really nice," he answered his wife, addressing everyone else at the same time. "Beth HaTalmud was most impressive and enjoyable."

"But I wasn't there with you!" Ariella reminded him with ersatz outrage.

"Oh, yes, well...in spite of your absence, dear. Services would have been unbearably wonderful had you been there."

Everyone laughed.

"Were any women there at all?" Ariella asked, circling slowly around the target she hoped to dive-bomb.

"You know, now that you mention it, I'm really not sure," Ovadyah replied hesitantly, surprised that he hadn't noticed. "I mean, if there were, I guess they were sitting behind the, the..."

"The *mechitzah*," Dina offered helpfully.

"The *mechitzah*," Ovadyah echoed, mentally recording the word.

Bull's-eye! thought Ariella as she cleared her throat. *Here I come!*

"Well," she observed aloud, "I guess they couldn't have felt very involved in the service if you couldn't even see them."

"I think Ovadyah was just saying that he didn't *notice* the women," Ron suggested politely, "that he was too engrossed in the service itself."

"Would you really *want* him noticing the women anyway?" Dina said, immediately surprised at herself. What had gotten *into* her?

Everyone laughed again, including Ariella. Then, for the first time that evening, Ed's wife, Susan, spoke up.

"I once attended services at an Orthodox synagogue," she recalled, "and not only did I feel isolated behind the partition, I felt belittled by being relegated to the back of the room."

"I'm sure you really did feel those things, Susan," Dina sympathized. "But were you *made* to feel them, or did you bring them to the synagogue with you? Many women are so sure they're going to be frustrated in shul that they bring all their frustrations along."

"All I know," Susan continued, undaunted, "is that I felt all alone, I missed Ed, and I could hardly see what was going on in the men's section."

"Uh, maybe I shouldn't talk," Ron said slowly, "never having sat behind the *mechitzah* myself, but, Susan, when you said you missed your husband, sitting so far from him, you made me think that maybe that was precisely why the Talmud mandates a separation between men and women at services. Maybe prayer is a time for focusing not on relationships with other people, but on God."

"You mean I'm supposed to forget about my wife when I pray?" Ed asked, one eyebrow raised almost to his hairline.

"Not forget *about* her," Ron explained. "I would hope she'd be an important subject of your prayers. But maybe you don't have to concentrate then on relating *to* her. There's a time for everything. Do you think about Susan when you're arguing a case?" He paused briefly for Ed's guilty chuckle. "Well," he continued, "prayer is a time for thinking about God."

"I take it back," Ed said. "You do make a good lawyer."

Having started the conversation, Ariella didn't like the way it was going so she decided to reenter it.

"Well I, for one, enjoy my husband's company at services. I don't find that sitting with my family inhibits my ability to pray meaningfully at all."

She had to admit to herself, though, that she wasn't sure it was true; she'd just never thought about it.

Ovadyah followed the conversation not only with his mind but with his head, oscillating like a spectator at a tennis match. He felt Ariella and Susan were being more strident than necessary, and not honest enough. He, too, enjoyed sitting with his wife at services, but he thought Ron's argument had some validity. After all, he'd felt a very special warmth at services that evening and Ariella hadn't even been in the building. He knew he couldn't fully enjoy a party or movie without Ariella, yet his prayers hadn't suffered for her absence. They may even have been more heartfelt than usual. In any event, he decided, this was certainly not the time to share his observations with Ariella.

"I just think we have to face the facts rather than try to justify them," Ariella continued, confirming the wisdom of Ovadyah's decision, "and the facts are that Orthodoxy, like most static religions, is generally patriarchal and unconcerned with women."

"Judaism has a long record of championing women's rights to security and safety," Dina interrupted agitatedly. "Did you know that two thousand years ago — two *thousand* years ago — the early Talmudic scholars instituted legal requirements to ensure that women would not be divorced and left without financial means?"

"So why did they require those same women to sit behind a wall during services?" Ariella asked, calmly but firmly.

"We suggested a reason for that before, Ariella," Ron reminded her. "It has everything to do with men's easily distracted minds and nothing to do with treating women badly."

Dina understood the assumptions Ariella was making and she knew they weren't true. She wasn't angry at her guest, just very frustrated.

"You really should talk to more Orthodox women," she told her. "You'd see that having a defined role doesn't mean you're a victim."

"Well, all I know is that I'll never allow our girls to be treated like second-class citizens. They'll get bat-mitzvahed, be called to read from the Torah, and be counted for a quorum just like any boy!"

"You'll be stroking their egos, all right," Dina said calmly, "but ignoring their true religious needs. Public Torah-reading isn't something you `get to do'; it's an *obligation* — and like all obligations, it has its rules and definitions."

"But how can you just accept the Orthodox rule that women can't participate?" Ariella pleaded in disbelief.

Dina didn't hesitate.

"The same way," she replied, "that I accept the biological fact that men cannot bear children. Or that women lack men's muscles. Or men, women's capacity for nurturing. *Roles*, Ariella. We have *roles* in life!"

"I like the model of an orchestra," Ron said quietly. "There are different instruments, each with a different part to play. It would be silly for the pianist to resent the tuba-player for having a louder, 'more prominent' sound. Each is equally important, equally essential, in spite of — actually, because of — their differences."

Ovadyah found that an interesting thought and made a mental note to discuss it at length with Ariella when she calmed down.

Meanwhile, the Waldmans' son, Josh, spoke up for the first time. Ovadyah and Ariella had almost forgotten he was there. Even the boy's parents seemed surprised to hear his voice.

"I don't know much about Jewish stuff, but what you just said reminded me of football. I used to wish I could be a quarterback, but I just didn't have the arm for it. And then one day I realized that being wide receiver wasn't 'second-rate' at all. I'm the fastest runner on the team and a good catcher — and *I* score the TDs! All of a sudden, I realized I wasn't less important than the quarterback, just different."

Ariella couldn't bring herself to argue with the earnest teen. He seemed like such a nice kid.

Dessert was served, and then the Waldmans excused themselves; Ed had to catch a plane the next morning. Ovadyah felt the frustration he always felt when a Jew showed a lack of respect for the Sabbath. It wasn't that he felt self-righteous, but he couldn't help but wonder how he, who hadn't even been born Jewish, was so careful not to violate the Sabbath, while so very many Jews whose biological ancestors had been meticulously observant seemed to feel little concern for perpetuating their past. He looked at Ron but saw no sign of pain on his face; he simply asked the departing guests if they wanted to say the grace after meals.

"Your *bentchers* have English translation, which is perfectly acceptable, and you can just read it quietly to yourselves."

After some hesitation, the guests spent several minutes doing just that. Then Ed closed his *bentcher*, followed by his wife and son, and thanked his hosts.

"A wonderful meal, Dina, and great company, too." Turning to Ovadyah and Ariella, he added, "It was a real pleasure meeting you folks. Have a good night, all! If I don't get to bed soon, I'll miss my 7:00 flight!"

Ovadyah winced but Ron just smiled at the Waldmans, shook Ed's hand, wished the family well and accompanied them to the door.

Ovadyah suspected that Ron hurt, too, but was just good at hiding it. He was right.

The girls were called to the table and Ron led his family and guests in reciting the first paragraph of the grace in Hebrew. Then the adults continued with the rest of the prayer by themselves. When everyone had finished, Ovadyah and Ariella excused themselves to get the twins ready for bed, Dina nursed the baby and Ron took care of Tanya.

Fifteen minutes later, the adults all found themselves together in the living room. Everyone felt like sitting down to talk, just for a few minutes and not about anything heavy; they'd had enough of that for one night. Dina left the room for a few minutes and returned with tea and sweets.

"So how do your kids like school?" she asked Ovadyah and Ariella as she set a tray down on the coffee table.

"Oh, they love it," Ovadyah answered, and Ariella nodded in agreement. "They're a little shy, but they've made friends and are getting good grades. And their Hebrew skills are better than ours!" Ron and Dina hadn't realized that the twins attended a Jewish school. So many Jewish parents, even those who were proud to be Jewish, simply chose the best private school they could find. They didn't seem to make the connection between their kids' Jewish identities and their education. The Rosens were therefore overjoyed to hear that the Gomeses had made a Jewish choice for their kids.

"They go to HHH?" Dina asked with surprise.

"No, to the Finkelstein School," Ariella replied.

Ron managed to hide his burst balloon. Dina was not as successful. She had never been a very good faker.

"Oh," she said, trying to fill what she thought was too long a silence. "Do they like it?"

"You asked us that before," Ariella pointed out. She hadn't taken her eyes off Dina and had seen her look of disappointment. "Is it because it's a Conservative day school that you don't like it?"
"Who said we don't like it?" Dina said with invented incredulity, an octave too high.

"Two witnesses," Ovadyah answered, alluding to the traditional legal requirement for testimony in a Jewish court. "Your eyes, when we said, `Finkelstein.'"

Dina had to laugh; both she and Ron blushed.

"It's not the school's affiliation," he explained, "so much as the quality of the Jewish education itself."

"What do you mean?" Ovadyah asked.

Ron realized that the relaxed, inconsequential conversation he had been looking forward to was just not to be. It seemed as if Providence had insisted that all the major Jewish issues of the times were to be aired that Shabbat with Ovadyah and Ariella. Ron decided it would be futile to fight it, so he jumped in headfirst.

For starters, he asked the Gomeses what their children studied at the Finkelstein School.

"Bible, Jewish ethics, Hebrew, and Jewish holidays," Ariella answered.

"And Jewish law?" Ron asked, fully aware that it wasn't in the curriculum.

"And are the holidays dealt with as obligations or just given lip service?" Dina chimed in.

"Is the Bible taught as revelation or as literature?" Ron added.

"Are the teachers model Jews, living what they teach?" It was Dina again this time.

"Whoa!" Ariella exclaimed. "One at a time!"

Though the first three questions had been troubling enough, the last one really hit hard. Only the previous Shabbat, while the Gomeses had been out for a walk, one of the children's teachers had driven by, honked a greeting and waved. They had realized, even as they'd sheepishly waved back, that the teacher had been the very one who had taught the girls about the sanctity of Shabbat. They had felt a curious mixture of embarrassment and anger.

"Okay," Ron said, his smile somehow punctuating his seriousness, "so why do you think Jewish law isn't taught?"

Ovadyah and Ariella tried their best to answer that and the other questions, but the Rosens were identifying many things that they themselves had been much bothered by but had been ignoring. After awhile, Ovadyah suddenly realized that he was feeling terribly tired. He glanced at his watch. It was just after 2:00 a.m.

CHAPTER 15

Unscheduled Departure

Ovadyah didn't have to take Ariella anywhere that Sunday; Shabbat had been anything but boring so she'd lost the bet. But when the twins were invited to a friend's house for the afternoon, the couple decided to go out anyway for a walk along a nearby river they often visited. It was an unusually brisk late-summer day and the sunshine, steady breeze and rushing water were conducive to clearing the mind. It seemed like a good time and place to take stock.

"Would you want to go back?" Ovadyah asked his wife.

Though his question had not been prefaced, she knew he was referring to the Rosens' farewell of the previous night. Their parting words had been ten percent "goodbye," ten percent "thanks for coming" and eighty percent "so when are you coming again?"

"I think so," Ariella answered.

"I wasn't sure. You did look like you were enjoying yourself, and I know I had a good time. But you sure seemed to want to pick a fight at times."

Ariella blushed.

"I don't know why I was so confrontational," she said, "but it wasn't because I didn't like Dina. Just the opposite. I like her a lot, and I respect her, too. But I just felt I had to challenge everything she stood for, at least with respect to women. I don't really know why."

"C'mon, Ariella, you've always been a feminist."

"But I never felt so motivated to argue my beliefs as I did over Shabbat."

Ovadyah paused, thought and finally spoke.

"Did you feel threatened by Dina?"

"Don't be silly. Threatened by what?"

"By her lifestyle and her beliefs. By her..." Ovadyah drifted off, deciding in mid-sentence that the word on his tongue would be too harsh. But he underestimated his wife's intuition.

"Success?" Ariella suggested.

An embarrassed look painted Ovadyah's face. Just then, a gull swooped down in front of them and glided away. It seemed to carry off some of his inhibition.

"Something like that," he admitted.

"I'm not sure," Ariella said with what her husband thought was surprising calm. "I don't *think* so. I mean, I don't envy her, though as I said, I *like* her. But I suppose she does present a challenge to the way I think."

They walked on quietly for several moments and then Ariella added, "What's really odd, though, is that the challenge she presents is part of what I like about her."

While Ovadyah hadn't felt threatened or challenged himself over the course of Shabbat, he understood what Ariella meant. And he was proud of her for meaning it.

He was happy, too, that he wouldn't have to fight with Ariella to spend more time with the Rosens. He had heartily enjoyed his Shabbat with the Orthodox family. He felt, for the first time, that he had witnessed Shabbat as he had seen it described in so many books over the years. And there could be no less pretentious people than the Rosens. They hadn't tried to overwhelm their guests, only to share their own Shabbat with them, to let them in on its beauty. And Ovadyah appreciated that, even though the beauty, at least of the services, had puzzled him.

It wasn't just Beth HaTalmud's spartan simplicity, its puniness in comparison to Beth Am. That he could understand; the simple is often more moving than the grandiose. But the decorum at services, the whole atmosphere at Beth HaTalmud, should have made him laugh in derision, not swell in fascination as he had. Not only had the services lacked the dark solemnity of the church he had attended as a youth, they hadn't even managed the basic dignity of Beth Am. People walked back and forth as they recited the prayers, unexpectedly chanting aloud any phrase they fancied, each worshipper out of sync with the other, not to mention out of tune. Small children ran underfoot and books lay in untidy piles everywhere. Yet Ovadyah had been inexplicably moved by the experience. Prayer there wasn't so much a ceremony as it was an essential human function, like eating or laughing — a natural expression of the congregants' Jewishness. For all its informality, the service had consisted of people talking to God. By contrast, he realized with a shock, the congregation at Beth Am seemed to be talking to itself.

The next day's mail brought a revelation. Spying an oversized manilla envelope bearing the Finkelstein School logo, Ariella figured, rightly, that it contained information about the coming year's curriculum and staff. As she skimmed the contents, Ovadyah watched his wife's expression change from curious to something like disgusted. Then, to his surprise, she angrily crumpled the paper and threw it to the floor.

"Wow!" he said simply.

"I've had enough" was her enigmatic explanation.

Ovadyah retrieved the paper, smoothed it out and saw it was a list of Finkelstein faculty members and their teaching credentials. He scanned the names; some were new, others he recognized from the previous year. None seemed in any way remarkable.

"Could you tell me what, uh, merited that reaction?" he asked, feeling as if he were tiptoeing through a minefield.

"Just look at the names!" she declared. "Don't you see what the entire religious staff has in common?"

"They're all women?" he asked cautiously.

"Well, in a way that's part of it," Ariella admitted, blushing, "but that's not the main thing."

"I give up," Ovadyah said abruptly, throwing delicacy to the wind.

"Not one is a rabbi!" Ariella exclaimed.

"So?"

"What do you mean, `So'? If they really cared about the religious end of their school, don't you think they'd have teachers with some religious credentials? Instead, they just leave the Judaic studies to whatever women they have sitting around!"

"Ariella?!" Ovadyah said with sufficient incredulity to convey his amazement at her seemingly sexist slur.

"I don't mean they're unqualified because they're women!" Ariella protested. "They're unqualified because they don't know anything about what they're teaching! If they were women rabbis, fine, but they're just Jewish general-studies teachers! And you know as well as I that women might be pampered and waved around by the rabbis at our synagogue, but they are hardly held in the highest regard."

Ovadyah hadn't known that at all, but now that he thought about it, much of the feminist rhetoric he had so often heard at Beth Am seemed a little hollow. The same condescension toward women he had all too often seen men display among themselves reigned unchallenged in the synagogue men's club. He supposed it did say something that only women taught the religious studies at the Finkelstein School even though none had any religious training.

"You wouldn't put even a good English teacher in front of a math class, would you?" Ariella went on, blending in with Ovadyah's thoughts. "And besides, you know most of those names. Not one of them is observant — and not one of them makes much effort to hide it. And that's who's going to teach our kids about living Judaism? I think that's what really galls me!"

The words set off a charge in Ovadyah's mind. He vividly recollected the Finkelstein School teacher who had cheerfully waved and honked to them the Shabbat before. It suddenly bothered him that he hadn't been equally outraged at the list of names.

"I guess Ron and Dina's points hit home," he finally said.

"Oh, c'mon, Ovadyah, you know perfectly well that this has been brewing for quite a while now. The more observant we've become, the more alone we've felt. You were as hurt as I was to see Mrs. Shamor merrily puttering around last Shabbat."

Ovadyah was startled by his wife's apparent mindreading.

"And more than a few of the other teachers openly talk about the non-kosher restaurants they frequent," Ariella continued. "Ron and Dina may have helped focus things, but you've got to admit that we've been down this road before."

Ovadyah knew she was right.

"What say we take the road all the way to its end this time?" he asked.

"You mean switch schools?"

"Uh-huh."

"But I'm president of the Parent-Teacher Association!"

"So?"

"I was hoping you'd see it my way!" Ariella exclaimed suddenly and with finality. "Will you make the arrangements?"

She couldn't help smiling inside; her husband, she realized, was likely in a state of shock from her ready acceptance of his suggestion.

"No problem," Ovadyah said confidently. He hadn't been surprised at all.

The next afternoon, Ovadyah sat in the waiting room outside Rabbi Solomon's office at Hope Heights Hebrew Day School. He felt at ease, especially after Ariella had described Rabbi Solomon as friendly and warm; she'd remembered visiting him on business two years earlier. Ovadyah figured that if the fellow had been nice to a salesperson, he would probably be downright lovable to the parent of two potential HHH students.

He wasn't disappointed. The rabbi came out of his office escorted his visitor in and sat him down in a comfortable chair. The place was every bit as disheveled as Ariella had recalled. Ovadyah wondered if the pile of papers on the rabbi's desk was the same one she had seen two years earlier. All in all, the place felt warm and homey, and Rabbi Solomon's broad smile accented the ambience.

"So I understand you're interested in our day school, Mr. Gomes," the rabbi began.

"Yes, very much so. Our twins are entering the second grade."

"And where have they been attending school until now?" the rabbi asked routinely.

"The Finkelstein School."

Rabbi Solomon's smile seemed to melt into his red beard. He always tried to maintain cordial relations between the two Jewish schools, a tricky balancing act considering that they stood for diametrical streams in Jewish life. Deep down, however, the rabbis and administrators at the Finkelstein School knew that Orthodoxy recognized no other Judaism. And Rabbi Solomon knew in turn that they had precious little love for things Orthodox, seeing traditional Judaism as some old, wealthy relative who not only refuses to bow out gracefully but insists on running marathons.

"Uh-huh" was all Rabbi Solomon said as he sized up the best way of saying what he felt had to be said. He figured he'd prod a bit first.

"Why don't you tell me, Mr. Gomes, why you want to switch schools?"

Not that the two places really had anything in common, he told himself. No two visions of Jewish education could be more divergent. He tried not to be judgmental when it came to the rival school but it was hard to stomach attempts to limit Judaism to social issues and arts and crafts.

In any event, any parents from the Finkelstein School who wanted to put their kids in Hope Heights Hebrew were probably "problem parents." Some people could be hopelessly blind when it came to their kids. If a child had some problem with a teacher or policy, or simply wasn't thriving in one school, parents would often just run to another — where the same thing usually happened again. Rabbi Solomon really didn't need such pointless, hopeless "defectors" in his school — especially if they'd defected from the Conservative crowd, he told himself. The Conservatives would accuse him of subversion and sowing discord before he could say, "Shalom aleichem."

"Well," Ovadyah began, "my wife and I have become increasingly observant over the past several years. We've stopped driving on Shabbat, other than to go to services..."

Rabbi Solomon squelched a flinch. What a sadly self-serving and groundless sanctioning of Sabbath-violation the Conservative movement had come up with when it decided to put Sabbath laws "on hold" in order to fill its sanctuaries. And this poor guy and his wife think it's a real exception to the law. How unfortunate, he thought. He really hurt for such people.

"...and we have a kosher home," Ovadyah continued, "and we are trying to study more about what observance entails."

What a pleasant guy he is, Rabbi Solomon observed, and what a shame he's probably not really Jewish. Most likely a Conservative convert, and the movement's attitude toward conversion laws resembled its approach to Sabbath laws. In the case of conversions, by compromising Jewish law, the Conservatives had created a subclass in the Jewish community: non-Jewish men and women who thought they were Jewish.

"That's very admirable of you. But why do you want to put your children in a different school?"

"Well, we're not really happy with the teachers at the Finkelstein School."

Here we go, thought Rabbi Solomon, another parent convinced that his kids' bad grades are the teachers' fault.

"What seems to be the problem?" he asked

"Well, they're not exactly role models for what they're teaching."

Huh? The rabbi did a double-take, though he tried not to let it show. He *cares*? It *bothers* him that Finkelstein's Judaic teachers are less than committed to a traditional Jewish lifestyle? Hey, who *is* this guy, anyway?

"In, uh, what way, Mr. Gomes, if I may ask?"

Ovadyah looked at the bearded man and wondered if the principal of a Jewish day school in Hope Heights could really be as naive as Rabbi Solomon seemed.

"Well, they're not Sabbath-observant, most of them. The men don't cover their heads and the women don't use the mikvah. And none of the staff are terribly well-educated in the texts and subjects they teach. The school just doesn't take religious studies as seriously as we'd like it to."

The rabbi was flabbergasted. This fellow Gomes has seen right through the Finkelstein School, he realized with amazement, right down to its staff's lack of commitment.

"We just can't see," Ovadyah continued, "how children exposed to Judaism in such an environment — even if it were taught well, which it isn't — could possibly come away with a real appreciation of the religion, and how they could possibly escape the process without a deep, lasting cynicism."

A happy shiver went down Mordechai Solomon's spine. This is unbelievable, this guy is something special, he told himself. But he made sure none of his enthusiasm leaked from his heart to his face. He couldn't be too careful when dealing with the Finkelstein School. If he in any way encouraged this fellow, the Finkelstein people would be on his case in ten minutes, accusing him of slandering their school and the entire Conservative movement. He didn't need that, especially when some of the most influential members of the local Jewish community took their marching orders directly from Rabbi Shoman.

Rabbi Solomon reminded himself how one overzealous rabbi on his staff was forever writing letters to the editor of the local Jewish paper, calling the Conservative movement to task for its lack of Jewish integrity. Each time a letter of his appeared, an outraged Rabbi Shoman would phone him and threaten to badmouth the school to some of its supporters who belonged to Beth Am. He would also demand that the letter-writer be forced to resign his teaching position. Rabbi Solomon usually managed to calm the clergyman down but always categorically refused to dismiss the teacher. He generally invoked the instructor's "right of free expression," something Rabbi Shoman always grudgingly acknowledged. But it was a real pain getting the calls and being threatened.

"Mr. Gomes," Rabbi Solomon finally said after pulling himself out of his thoughts, "I really think you need to proceed slowly and cautiously here. I wouldn't want you to do anything you might later regret. Are you sure you can't deal with this by talking to Rabbi Allen or Rabbi Shoman? Maybe some changes can be made in the staff or curriculum at the Finkelstein School."
"Rabbi Solomon," Ovadyah explained, almost pleading, "please trust me. I know what I'm talking about, and believe me, there is no hope for the type of fundamental change that would be necessary. It's not that we don't like the people at Beth Am or the Finkelstein School. We have many friends among the congregants and parents, and even among the teachers. We just want our girls to get a real Jewish education. I'm the *gabbai* at Beth Am and my wife is the president of the Finkelstein School PTA. I think we know the school fairly well."

The rabbi nearly swallowed his tongue on hearing about Ovadyah and Ariella's positions in the Conservative community. Oh no, he thought, why did *this* have to land in my lap? This man's no small fry, he's the *gabbai* at Beth Am! They'll have his head, not to mention mine, if he switches schools!

Rabbi Solomon smiled benevolently at his guest — he'd long since learned how to keep panic from showing — and calmly said, "You mentioned the friends you have at Beth Am. Do you realize the, uh, impact your decision will have on those relationships?"

He remembered a similar case several years earlier. Parents who had transferred their kids from the Finkelstein School to Hope Heights Hebrew had been so ostracized and tormented by their friends, who'd accused them of stabbing the Conservative school in the back, that in the middle of the school year they abruptly re-enrolled their children in the Finkelstein School.

"Rabbi," Ovadyah said patiently, "you don't seem to understand. We're talking about our children's education and future as Jews. Anything that might happen as a result of our concern for our kids, we'll just have to learn to live with. Besides, any friends who would shun us for that concern really aren't very good friends to begin with. Right now, all that matters is the Jewish education our kids receive. Will you accept them?"

Rabbi Solomon took a deep breath.

"Mr. Gomes," he said, suddenly very serious, "if you're sure you want your children in Hope Heights Hebrew, we'll work something out. But first please tell me, are you and your wife born Jews?"

"My wife is, and I'm a *ger*," Ovadyah said.

Rabbi Solomon was relieved to know he wouldn't have to enter into the whole business of the status of the Conservative movement's conversions in the eyes of Orthodoxy. Jewish law considers the mother's Jewishness to be the sole determinant of a child's status as a Jew. He couldn't in good conscience enroll a non-Jewish child in the school but, thankfully, the Gomes children were indisputably Jewish.

"I see. And are you certain you want to switch your kids so abruptly, right before school starts? I mean, maybe you'd rather set your sights on next year."

"No, we want to move them now," came the quick answer.

Rabbi Solomon made no effort to force the issue — nor, now, to stop his happiness from spreading over his face like a sunburst. There was no mistaking the rabbi's honest goodwill as he clasped Ovadyah's hand tightly and said, "Mr. Gomes, it has been a real honor to meet you."

CHAPTER 16

Changing Times

W hat?" Rabbi Allen said, uncomprehending. "Well, we've become concerned about certain areas of the kids' education, and we think we'll be able to gain more somewhere else."

He had heard right, the Finkelstein School principal told himself. This man sitting before him, who only months before hadn't even been Jewish, whose very skin proclaimed his recent arrival, was actually telling an ordained rabbi and noted educator that he had outgrown the Louis Finkelstein Jewish School, "a state-of-the-art educational institution in the best tradition of Conservative Judaism, the largest branch of Judaism in America" — in the words of the full-color brochure he liked to show parents.

"I'm afraid I don't understand," he said quite honestly.

Ovadyah took a deep breath. He had known this wouldn't be easy.

"It's a little hard to explain," he began, though it really wasn't, not if he could have spoken more bluntly than he felt he should. "It's not so much that we're uncomfortable at the Finkelstein School. We're generally happy with our children here, but our lifestyle has evolved somewhat and we want the kids' education to be in line with the way we're living. We want their growth to parallel our own."

Ovadyah realized that he'd been pretty blunt after all. And it showed in Rabbi Allen's face, which had metamorphosed from uncomprehending to pained and almost hurt.

This was not going well, Ovadyah thought. He and Ariella had hoped not to lose their Finkelstein School friends as a result of their move to Hope Heights Hebrew, but if Rabbi Allen couldn't understand their concerns, chances were that their friends wouldn't, either.

"We really don't want you or anyone else to be upset with us. We still belong to Beth Am and value all our friends here," Ovadyah continued. "It's just that we feel we have to act in our kids' best educational interests."

Why did everything he tried to say seem to come out sounding like an insult, Ovadyah asked himself in frustration.

He recalled how he and Ariella had discussed the possibility of some folks not being able to handle their "defection" from the Finkelstein School. He had asked his wife what she would say if any of their friends suddenly became cold to them. "Tough," she'd said tersely. Though Ovadyah had thought she was being hasty, he had since come to agree that any friends who would begrudge them their educational standards for their children were no great friends to begin with. Still, he wanted to cushion their move. If something could be done in a friendly way, he felt, why make a confrontation of it?

"Listen, Ovadyah," Rabbi Allen said after a moment, "I really think you're making a big mistake."

"How's that?" Ovadyah replied, sounding more like Sergeant Friday than he had intended.

"Well," Rabbi Allen began hesitantly, "why HHH, of all places?"

"I tried to tell you before. It's just more in line with the way we've chosen to live. I want my kids to know the laws of Shabbat, not just some songs and customs. And I want them to hear that non-kosher food isn't acceptable for Jews to eat."

"Well, as you well know," Rabbi Allen interrupted with a note of chagrin, "the Conservative movement most certainly does consider the laws of Shabbat and *kashrut* very important. We simply recognize a need to apply ancient laws to modern times in a reasoned and intelligent manner. That's certainly no reason to opt out of our school!"

"Rabbi," Ovadyah said calmly, "I hear it but I don't see it. Not only are the kids not really taught anything about the laws of Judaism, some of their teachers have no regard for those laws, either. You know as well as I that you have teachers who eat at non-kosher restaurants and ignore many of the Sabbath laws. How can you fault us for wanting more observant, committed teachers for our children?"

Ovadyah delivered the last line with some hurt in his voice, in the hope that, despite the harshness of his indictment, some goodwill might still be salvaged.

Yet Rabbi Allen was outraged at Ovadyah's apparent haughtiness. Just because this congregant has chosen to keep kosher and observe Shabbat, he thought to himself, he thinks he can impugn the religious convictions of others who have made different choices! Rabbi Allen had known converts to have unrealistic expectations at times, and even to undertake unnecessary observances, but never had he seen one so utterly intolerant. He decided to ignore Ovadyah's words altogether.

"What I really think you're overlooking," he said earnestly, "is that you're not moving *up* from a less Jewish school to a more Jewish one. You're simply moving *out*, away from — let's face it, Ovadyah — the only stream of Judaism with a future. Hope Heights Hebrew is an *Orthodox* school. Don't forget that. There may be other children of Beth Am members there but that doesn't change the fact that the faculty and philosophy of the place are unquestionably Orthodox. Do you really want your kids exposed to that? You're actually moving backwards, Ovadyah, and I'm worried about you. The Orthodox like to call themselves 'Torah Jews,' but I would think you've learned enough about Conservative Judaism to know that it alone represents the true spirit of Judaism. Orthodoxy is a fossil. They can shake it at your kids all they like but it's just an old bag of dry bones."

The rabbi felt he had chosen an appropriately strong and clever metaphor, but Ovadyah was only reminded of the "dry bones" that miraculously came together before Ezekiel's eyes and lived anew.

"Well, I do appreciate your input, and I wish our decision weren't necessary, but unfortunately we've had to do what we've done. We're not leaving Beth Am, only the Finkelstein School. We hope you won't take it personally."

"I certainly won't," Rabbi Allen said. "I care too much for you and Ariella to do that, but that's precisely why I still wish you'd reconsider. I really think you'll regret this."

He gathered his thoughts, then quickly added, "And just think of the impact on other parents — especially considering that you're the *gabbai* and your wife's the PTA president!" He paused a moment as the full implication of the couple's decision became apparent. "Or should I say, past president."

"That is unfortunate," Ovadyah admitted, "but we do have to make our children's welfare our prime concern. I know you agree with me on that."

"Of course," the rabbi replied, as he knew he must, "though what's best for them is not necessarily the plan you have in mind."

"Maybe not, but that has to be our decision as parents."

Realizing the futility of further discussion, Rabbi Allen pasted a polite smile over his frown. Ovadyah Gomes had obviously closed his mind to any alternatives, so there was no point in wasting more time trying to dissuade him.

Their decision to move the twins to Hope Heights Hebrew Day School seemed to embolden Ovadyah and Ariella to act on something else that had been troubling them. Though the legal authorities in the Conservative movement had sanctioned the use of automobiles on the Sabbath for the purpose of attending services, the Gomeses had grown uncomfortable about driving anywhere on Shabbat. It felt odd engaging in an activity that was otherwise prohibited. Furthermore, the Torah clearly forbade combustion, so the allowance to drive to synagogue was just that — an allowance, a necessary evil. Finally, the fact that very few members of the congregation distinguished between "permitted" and "non-permitted" driving made the couple wonder about the wisdom of the movement's ruling to begin with.

So, rather than capitulate to the majority, something their religious sensitivities would never allow them to do, Ovadyah and Ariella stopped driving on the Sabbath altogether. This meant that unless they stayed with friends who lived near Beth Am, they could not attend services on Shabbat. It also meant that Ovadyah's position as *gabbai* was effectively resigned. And it meant that even acquaintances at Beth Am who had managed to accept that the Gomes children were now in an Orthodox school wondered whether their model "Jew by choice" and his family had gone entirely off the deep end, becoming religious fanatics — Conservative religious fanatics, but religious fanatics just the same.

Indeed, at one synagogue meeting shortly thereafter, a very serious and well-meaning congregant warned Ariella to "be careful" now that she and Ovadyah were "involved with the Hebrew Day School crowd, not to get brainwashed" by their new friends. Ariella thanked her tersely for her concern.

None of their friends showed any ill will toward them in their presence, though, and they continued to attend functions at Beth Am. Ovadyah remained a weekday regular at the "upstairs minyan," and both he and Ariella still participated in the adult education program. But at the same time, they were broadening their circle of friends and acquaintances, meeting other, often Orthodox people with whom they occasionally spent Shabbat.

Both Ovadyah and Ariella tried to increase their study of Judaism in other ways, too. Books were fine, but they felt that a certain human element was needed, if only for discussion and clarification. The classes at Beth Am had become tiresome and, they now realized, had never really been wholly satisfying. Rabbi Sinsky's class was different; they felt he had something of substance to teach, whereas the other courses consisted of either dry, lifeless study of "ancient texts" for their historical rather than inherent value, or touchy-feely psychobabble.

Once they went to a special "discussion group" at Beth Am on the topic of prayer. Rabbi Shoman himself was to lead the group, so they felt it might be time well-invested.

"What I want us to do tonight," Rabbi Shoman opened the proceedings after the twenty-odd people in attendance had seated themselves around a large table, "is to come to a deeper understanding of prayer in Jewish life. The best way for us to do this is by sharing our experiences and insights with each other."

Ovadyah and Ariella actually cared more for what Jewish tradition had to say about prayer than about their fellow congregants' feelings on the matter, but they figured the rabbi would eventually get to that. He never did, though.

Instead, he went around the table asking each person what prayer meant to him or her. The responses were so subjective and trivial that Ovadyah turned to his wife to see her reaction. Noticing his glance, Ariella just looked heavenward in an exaggerated but barely noticeable gesture of frustration. He was glad to see that she seemed similarly unimpressed.

One man told how a few moments' meditation each afternoon helped him clear his head and have a more productive final few hours at work. He seemed to Ovadyah to be extolling the virtue of "prayer" as an aid in stockbroking. Another person said that talking to God in her mind throughout the day made her feel better about the decisions she made. Well, that's a little closer, thought Ariella; at least God was part of her report. On and on the testimonies came, each one a heartfelt description of how prayer — or something similar — "helped" the supplicant. The rabbi nodded sagely throughout, never once asking if prayer meant anything to anyone beyond a psychological boost. It was as if the group saw value in the experience only insofar as it might help one make more money, be a more effective manager of time and people, or just feel good. Ovadyah couldn't help thinking that he had been foolish to imagine Rabbi Shoman having anything to teach him about prayer; he couldn't remember the last time the rabbi had shown up at daily services.

Fortunately, though, Ovadyah and Ariella's thirst for knowledge could be indulged in other ways. For instance, Ron and Dina had offered to set up *chavrusos* with them. As the Gomeses understood it, a *chavrusah* — the Aramaic form of the Hebrew word meaning "friend" — meant a personalized study pair. Ron and Ovadyah would sit together and work on a text, Dina and Ariella doing the same at a different time of the day. Each member of the study pair would benefit from the other's experience, language skills, intelligence or creativity. It made for a hands-on and efficient means of gleaning both information and familiarity with the text under study.

The men decided to tackle daily laws like the ritual washing of hands in the morning, tefillin and the laws of prayer itself. Ovadyah hadn't realized how a Jew's every act was so governed by minute laws and customs. Some people, he imagined, would probably find that constricting and overwhelming. But he felt that it gave him constant direction, reminding him that there was a right and wrong way to do everything in life, that nothing in human sphere was too trivial to include God and His will.

Ariella and Dina opted to study about prayer and niddah, the "family purity" laws.

Ovadyah also came across a remarkable book that impressed him greatly. It wasn't really about Judaism per se at all. It was a sociological study of something it called the "yeshivah world," the subculture of Orthodox rabbinical students. He hadn't known one existed. The book painted a vivid picture of dedicated Jews studying Torah in order to better serve God. Few of those in yeshivah were even interested in the rabbinate. Most wanted either to teach, or simply to study as much as they could before embarking on a career. Ovadyah was amazed to read of such a vital segment of Orthodox Jewry. These people, he thought were like a living remnant of the Eastern European Jewry he had read so much about, whose culture he thought had perished in the Holocaust. To be sure, the rabbinical students were hardly stuck in the past; the study made clear that they lived, without question, in the twentieth century, often struggling with the implications of that fact. But their familiarity with modernity, and their accommodation of it, in no way diminished their ideals and commitment, which were ancient — and vibrantly Jewish.

What most struck Ovadyah about what he came to recognize as the heart of Orthodoxy was the emphasis on constant study by means of *chavrusos*, the same "learning partner" arrangement he had with Ron. The knowledge that there were thousands of study pairs like his own, all studying the Jewish texts he himself wanted to explore, was a revelation to him.

The bulk of this study centered on the Talmud, the encyclopedic work that formed the bedrock of

Judaism. It was a work Ovadyah had sampled only selectively and occasionally. Rabbi Shoman had given a seminar once, consisting of five lectures on Talmudic selections. But the rabbi had treated the books of the Talmud as quaint historical curiosities, not living guides for Jews today. Rabbi Shoman had performed an intellectual autopsy for his students, rather than displaying a healthy patient. Yet in dozens of yeshivos, it seemed, thousands of young Jewish scholars were learning Talmud as if their lives depended on understanding its every implication and message. Ovadyah shared his excitement with Ariella, as always, and both felt encouraged to learn more about Judaism, to pursue every path they found. At least they knew that, no matter how it seemed, they were not alone.

When they spent Shabbat with the Rosens, they would attend services either at Beth HaTalmud or at B'nei Yeshurun, another Orthodox congregation in the neighborhood. Sometimes there were study groups or classes at one or another of the synagogues, often exclusively for men or women, and Ovadyah and Ariella appreciated the additional opportunities for furthering their Jewish education.

Once, Ariella accompanied Dina to an informal lecture given on Shabbat by one of the teachers at Hope Heights Hebrew. The lecture concerned the weekly Torah portion read in the synagogue that morning. Though the rabbi spoke in perfectly grammatical and unaccented English, Ariella had trouble understanding him since he peppered every sentence with Hebrew phrases. She wondered if the other women were having similar difficulty with the lecture, and if any were, why they didn't interrupt the teacher for clarification when he lapsed into Hebrew. She certainly wasn't going to do so; she'd never even been to one of these things before. So she just listened as attentively as she could and tried to catch the gist of what the rabbi was saying.

He was speaking about some ritual that he called "the ultimate *chok*." Thankfully, he explained right at the start that a *chok* was "a Torah law with no discernible logical, sociological, moral or historical meaning." That concept bothered Ariella a lot. She didn't see why anything had to be beyond explanation. Everything she had studied about Judaism and Jewish law had stressed the *meaning* of Jewish practices, and even though the specifics of observances were sometimes hard to square with the theory behind them, at least some general reasoning was put forth for the commandments and laws. But this rabbi was saying certain things not only were not explained, but could not be explained — even things that seemed, to human logic, self-contradictory. She didn't like that.

But what irked her even more was the passive way the women in attendance let him get away with everything he said. There was no interaction at all between the lecturer and the lectured. The women just sat there listening. Certain points the rabbi made seemed to register on their faces, but none of them challenged anything he said. After he finished speaking, several women finally did ask some questions, but they were only requests for further clarification; not one took issue with him in any way.

Walking home with Dina, Ariella related her impressions.

"Well, I think that was the rabbi's very point," Dina responded, "that certain things in Torah, just like in life and nature, are simply beyond our understanding. He didn't say that it sits well with us humans, only that it was true. I think you *should* feel the frustration you do about the concept, at least at first. But what he was saying was that we've also got to realize how little we really do understand, even when we think we've grasped it all."

Ariella heard her point, though her mind still balked at the notion of laws for people without any connection to human comprehension.

"I guess all he was saying," she said after a moment, "was that God knows more about what's best for humans than we do ourselves, so certain of His instructions are bound to be puzzling to us."

"No less than ours are to our children," Dina added.

When they reached Dina's house, Ariella mentioned the other thing that had bothered her about the *shiur*.

"Why didn't any of the women give him an argument about anything?" she asked.

"An argument?" Dina repeated. "They weren't there to argue. They were there to learn."
Ariella needed some time to think about that one.

CHAPTER 17

Vital Information

Joe Winkler had challenged Ovadyah's assumptions. Joe was one of the new acquaintances he and Ariella had made over the months since they had entered the Rosens' circle of friends. The Winklers were nice people, Ovadyah knew, and Joe would never say anything to hurt him — goodness, he'd only *known* him for a few weeks! Which made Joe's suggestion smart all the more.

They were at a bar mitzvah at B'nei Yeshurun — the Orthodox shul to which the Winklers belonged — and had been talking about the differences between their respective houses of worship.

Joe hadn't intended the comment to be incendiary; it had just seemed the obvious thing to say, the almost predictable conclusion to their conversation. But his discomforting words hit ground zero deep in Ovadyah's heart and the searing fallout slowly spread to his consciousness.

"You know," Joe pointed out, "if you converted Orthodox, you could join B'nei Yeshurun."

If I converted Orthodox?! Ovadyah choked on the phrase for an instantaneous eternity, passing through successive palls of puzzlement, anger and insult. *I've already converted to Judaism,* he reassured himself. *If I wanted to become Orthodox, I'd only have to...become Orthodox! I wouldn't need to convert again!* He decided to ignore Joe's comment — for the moment, anyway. Ovadyah really liked Joe; he had found him polite, friendly and caring. Honest, too, and that, he quickly realized, was what really bothered him. Joe had been speaking sincerely, without pretensions. The guy, Ovadyah thought with the mental equivalent of a nervous smile, actually *believed* that a Conservative convert would not be allowed to join an Orthodox congregation!

He wondered if it were true.

Over the next few days, mulling the idea over, Ovadyah had to admit that it did explain a few things.

For instance, while Mr. Finch, the elderly director of Beth Am's "upstairs minyan," had always been friendly to him, Ovadyah had come to sense something odd about the way the man acted toward him, in particular with regard to the leading of services. Ovadyah's Hebrew skills had developed nicely over the months, evidence of all the work he had put in, and he often led the Sabbath services in the main sanctuary. Yet Mr. Finch never allowed him to do the same for the daily minyan, the "traditional" one.

Could it be, Ovadyah now thought, that Mr. Finch didn't consider his own rabbi's conversions valid? He knew that Mr. Finch was more observant than almost anyone else in the congregation, and that he had been raised Orthodox. But the man was, after all, a ritual director in a Conservative synagogue! Could he really play both sides of the game like that?

Ovadyah decided, after several weeks of wondering, to simply confront Mr. Finch and ask him if he was trying to keep converts from leading the services. Mr. Finch registered great surprise at the query and assured his questioner that he was doing nothing of the sort. But Ovadyah didn't believe him.

Ovadyah even considered talking to Rabbi Shoman about his suspicions but then thought better of it, especially when Mr. Finch finally allowed him to lead the first part of the service one day. It was just the portion of preliminary Psalms but it did say something, Ovadyah felt...sometimes. But there was something else, too, that suddenly started making equally uncomfortable sense.

Ovadyah enjoyed attending services in different synagogues. One week he'd go to Beth HaTalmud, another to B'nei Yeshurun, the following week to a third shul, Anshei Emunah. He was always cordially welcomed and soon stopped feeling self-conscious about being the only non-Caucasian and the only Conservative Jew — and certainly the only non-Caucasian Conservative Jew — in attendance. After several months, however, he noticed a disturbing pattern: He wasn't being counted in the minyan, the quorum of ten men required for Jewish communal prayer!

Usually, each shul had more than ten men for services so there was no way for Ovadyah to know if he was being counted toward the quorum. Sometimes, though, even when there seemed to be a quorum in attendance, he saw the rabbi rush to the phone to call someone else to come.

And now, after Joe's innocently outrageous question, Ovadyah knew nearly for certain what he had refused to let himself think outright until then: To Orthodox Jews, it seemed, he simply wasn't Jewish.

His first thoughts were angry ones. How dare anyone doubt my sincerity, Ovadyah grumbled to himself. But after several days of reflection, he realized that his sincerity was not likely the problem in Orthodox eyes. What was missing from his conversion was probably just what he himself had come to feel was missing from the movement that had converted him: full commitment to Jewish law. He wasn't sure what made Conservative conversions invalid in the Orthodox view, but he had learned enough about both Halachah and the Conservative movement to know that there was probably something to the Orthodox objections.

Disappointment and frustration rained from the cloud of his dissipating anger. He had no clear course of action other than to try to understand things better, to plumb Orthodoxy's attitude toward his conversion, his status, and toward Conservatism itself.

Meanwhile, Rosh HaShanah was less than two weeks away; Ovadyah and Ariella had arranged to spend it in the Rosens' neighborhood. The holiday was destined, at least in some small way, to bring things together for them.

After services on the second day of Rosh HaShanah, the Gomeses and Rosens walked the half-mile back to Ron and Dina's house together. It was a glorious, early autumn day, the colors of the new fall playing in summer's warm lap like a glittering grandchild. As they walked, Ron informed his guests that another family would be joining them for lunch.

"Who are they?" Ariella asked.

"The Shafrans," Dina answered. "He's a rabbi — teaches at Hope Heights Hebrew — and she's a full-time mother."

When they reached the house, Ovadyah and Ariella saw that Dina's description of Mrs. Shafran had been no exaggeration. Waiting near the porch steps was a thirtyish couple — the man with a bigger beard than suited his face, the woman wheeling a stroller back and forth to comfort the baby boy it held — and four little girls, the eldest perhaps six years old, running circles around their parents.

"They're really nice people," Dina continued while they were still out of earshot of the waiting family.

In fact, the compliment was most accurate for the female half of the couple. The rabbi could be a bit strident at times, and had something of a reputation for belligerence, especially when it came to countering the claims of the non-Orthodox movements. He wrote a lot of magazine articles and letters to the editors of the local press, and his defenses of Orthodoxy often came down quite hard on other branches of Judaism. Rabbi Shoman had utter contempt for him and had repeatedly tried to have him dismissed from Hope Heights Hebrew.

Dina, of course, didn't mention any of that; she didn't dwell on the negative when it came to people. The Torah, she knew, had laws governing speech — just as it governed every other action — and those laws prohibited in no uncertain terms any gratuitous "badmouthing" of others.

Dina knew that Rabbi Shafran felt he was doing the Jewish people a vital service by exposing what he felt were spiritually dangerous trends. She was also sure that he would recognize the sensitivity of the situation once he was introduced to the Gomeses, and that he would act accordingly.

Ron and Dina had felt for some time that it would be interesting to get the Shafrans and the Gomeses together. The latter were full of questions and the former, being children and grandchildren of devout Orthodox Jews, and having received extensive Jewish educations, were better prepared to provide answers than Ron and Dina felt they were themselves. It might also be

110

interesting, the hosts had reasoned further, to expose Ovadyah and Ariella to people who minced no words about the state of the modern Jewish community, who didn't hesitate to challenge the assumptions of the average American Jew, and who could do so with the support of Jewish history and sources.

Once the holiday meal got under way, Ron got the conversation going with several questions he had about the idea of a Jewish new year. Rabbi Shafran may not have chosen the pulpit but he seemed to fancy himself a pulpit rabbi, delivering a veritable sermon in response to each query. And Mrs. Shafran combined her husband's erudition with a quiet demeanor, saying much even as she spoke little. Ovadyah felt there was a lot to be learned from the pair, and he paid close attention to all that was said. He saw Ariella doing the same.

Somehow the topic of discussion turned to something Rabbi Shafran was calling "pluralism," by which he meant modern Judaism's split into Orthodox, Conservative and Reform groups. The rabbi didn't care for it.

Never one to allow self-consciousness to interfere with learning, Ovadyah asked the rabbi if Orthodoxy didn't itself subscribe to a plurality of approaches.

"The Talmud is full of argument, isn't it?" he asked softly, pointedly, sincerely.

The rabbi then launched into what seemed a stock speech on the validity of varied approaches, but within the "framework of Torah," as he put it. He told a long story about some great rabbi predicting that the Mormons would start accepting blacks before they actually did, though the others weren't sure what he was getting at. Finally, many words later, he returned to the subject. His point, it eventually became clear to Ovadyah and Ariella, was that the litmus test of "legitimate pluralism" was whether the divergent approaches were truly dedicated to advancing God's revealed will, or engineered only to yield preconceived conclusions.

It was a good point, the Gomeses both admitted to themselves, one that struck squarely home, colliding full force with their memories of how Jewish law was treated at Beth Am.

"But at what point," Ovadyah asked, "does an emphasis on the needs of modern man go from legitimate concern, from what you call the `framework of Torah,' to what you would consider an illegitimate digression from God's will?"

"Well, that's a rather involved subject," the rabbi responded, "but there's really little need to split hairs if you're just trying to judge whether the Conservative and Reform movements are loyal to what has historically been called Torah. They don't even subscribe to the *event* of the Revelation, much less to the vitality of its content!"

"That's not true," Ariella earnestly contended. "The Reform movement may reject the authenticity of Torah, but we're Conservative Jews and we take the idea of Sinai quite seriously."
"Well, you might indeed," the rabbi acknowledged, "but your movement doesn't require that of its members — or of its rabbis, for that matter! So, individuals aside, the Conservative *system* allows for a rejection of the historicity of Sinai, the very bedrock of what has always been called Judaism. How can a movement that allows the entire source of Torah to be mythologized possibly call itself Judaism? Jewish, perhaps, since it is largely composed of Jews. But *Judaism*?

I'm sorry. Not every Jewish movement is Judaism."

"What do you mean by that?" Ron interjected.

"Well, Christianity was a Jewish movement at first. Socialism was, too, in a way. Secular Zionism is Jewish, but certainly not identical to Judaism."

Ovadyah frowned almost imperceptibly. Was this rabbi comparing the Conservative movement to *Christianity*? That was ridiculous. He suddenly heard Dina give voice to his thoughts, challenging the rabbi's comparison.

"I'm not making an actual point-to-point comparison," Rabbi Shafran explained. "I'm just pointing out that a Jewish group's rejection of any fundamental element of Judaism, whether its messiah or its historical foundation, separates it from the Judaism of the ages. You might think it crazy but the way things are headed, Orthodox Jews won't even be able to regard the non-Orthodox as *Jews* within several generations!"

"Why is that?" Ariella asked, disgust dripping from her words like tanker oil from a seabird. Rabbi Shafran hesitated, realizing the conceptual corner — considering his audience — he'd painted himself into. Ovadyah understood, though.

"What he means, dear," he explained quietly to his wife, "is that the more converts the non-Orthodox make, the more non-Jews — as the Orthodox see them — there will be in Conservative and Reform circles."

The rabbi's uncharacteristic silence affirmed the explanation.

"But Rabbi," Ovadyah continued, seizing the chance, "what exactly is it about, say, a Conservative conversion that makes it unacceptable to the Orthodox?"

Rabbi Shafran found his tongue. Much to the despair of some who found themselves in his company, it was seldom lost for long.

"Actually, such conversions lack one or more of the requirements of Jewish law."

"Well, I had a *hatafah*," Ovadyah informed the rabbi, recalling the symbolic drawing of circumcision blood, "and I went to the *mikvah*."

"But was there a clear declaration," he asked, "that commandments, requirements, exist in Judaism and govern every facet of life? And did you accept them all, sight unseen, so to speak, undertaking to fulfill each of them to the best of your ability?"

"Well," Ovadyah responded, "I think I understood that on my own."

"You were never told, though, as you were about to enter the *mikvah*, that you had to accept mitzvot?"

Ovadyah suppressed a cynical snicker. "I don't think I was ever told at *any* point," he confessed, almost to himself.

"Well, now you know what is lacking in Conservative conversions, not to mention Reform ones. Insistence on *kabbalat hamitzvot*, on the acceptance of all the commandments in principle, is no mere icing on the cake. It's the essence of conversion. And it is something that the Conservative and Reform movements can hardly in good faith require from converts, since they don't even embrace the concept themselves!"

"Has the law always required this acceptance?" Ron asked. "I mean, is it clearly written in the Jewish legal texts?"

"Unmistakably," the rabbi replied, adding with sarcasm, "though some rabbis' books seem to be missing those lines."

Ovadyah was reeling from what the rabbi had said. He knew full well that the vast majority of converts at Beth Am converted solely to marry Jews, and that even those who accepted the label "Jew" wholeheartedly did so without the slightest notion of *commandments*, or requirements incumbent on Jews. To them, Judaism was at best a moral mission, and more often a mere social system; they were simply joining the Jewish "club." Paying one's synagogue dues was the only real sacrifice required.

"But again," Ovadyah asked pointedly, "what about a Conservative convert who did recognize the importance of mitzvot? What would be wrong with his or her conversion?"

"Well," Rabbi Shafran responded, fully aware of the personal import of his answer, "theoretically, perhaps nothing. But that is a rare case. And in any event, there is still the question of the witnesses' acceptability. According to Halachah, conversion, like marriage or any other legal transition, requires the presence of witnesses. Anyone who has rejected authentic Judaism may not serve this intrinsic function."

Ovadyah pressed the rabbi on that point, trying to ascertain just whom Orthodoxy would consider to have "rejected authentic Judaism," but Rabbi Shafran seemed reluctant to get specific, subtly changing the subject to Israeli politics when no one was listening. Undaunted, Ovadyah decided to change the subject again himself. If the guy's going to talk so much, he figured, let him at least talk about something I want to know about. So he interrupted the ongoing discourse on Knesset machinating and asked the rabbi how he would argue for the truth of Judaism's historical tradition, how he knew that the revelation at Sinai actually took place.

In a long-winded but lucid lecture, the rabbi argued that historical truth was established only through the mass witnessing of events. He then showed how Judaism was based on the mass witnessing of God's revelation by the entire Jewish people, who perpetuated the event just as we do the history of our own times, by passing it on as sacred tradition to the next generation. Thus, Judaism could claim for the revelation at Sinai the same historical veracity claimed for the fall of Rome or the World Wars. Only Judaism, he continued, could make such a claim, for only it began with a mass experience, unlike Christianity or Islam, each of which was founded by an individual who simply convinced others of his own *personal* "revelation."

The children had long since gone off to play in another part of the house and the Rosens' dining room seemed to have entered some strange dimension where time existed only when the clock was consulted. The sun had ignored the tiny time warp of the holiday meal, though, and was descending toward late afternoon. When the noise from where the children were playing began to intrude on the dining-room conversation, the parents called their kids, everyone recited the grace after meals together, and the Shafrans, after thanking their hosts for the meal and for the pleasure of meeting the Gomeses, bid their goodbye, wishing everyone a blessed year and receiving the same blessings in return.

When they had gone, Ovadyah turned to the others and said, "Well now, that was an interesting meal!"

"I thought you'd enjoy meeting the Shafrans," Dina said. "You can learn a lot from them if you want to."

"I'm not sure we wanted to learn all we did," Ariella said with a pained smile.

She wasn't sure if it was Mrs. Shafran's full-time motherhood and the ease with which she dealt with her large family, or Rabbi Shafran's bluntness, but something stuck like a thorn in her brain. She saw that Ovadyah, too, despite his comment, seemed troubled. It was getting late, though, so rather than pursue things then and there, Ariella reminded her husband that they were expected back at the Weinmans', where they were staying.

As they summoned the twins and began to take their leave, however, Ovadyah asked Ron where the Shafrans lived.

"Just a few blocks away, on Prospect Street. Why?"

"Oh, I just wanted to ask the rabbi one more question. I thought maybe we could just stop there for a few minutes on the way home."

"Well, it's certainly not very much out of your way," Ron said. "And I'm sure they'll be happy to see you again, even so soon."

He was right.

CHAPTER 18

Broken Home

S
o what've I got scheduled this morning, Cindy?" Rabbi Solomon grumbled, barely glancing in his secretary's direction as he headed toward his office.

He had arrived at school late that cold, February morning — car trouble — only to find that the second-floor ceiling was leaking even though it hadn't rained or snowed in over a week. Then, just as he passed a pale, anxious-looking kindergartner in the school lobby, the child suddenly lost his breakfast all over the floor. It was going to be one of those days, the rabbi thought as he tried without success to calm the little boy, one of those days when the mandatory smiles for teachers and staff would strain even his considerable interpersonal skills. He had managed a pleasant, grateful one for the teacher who relieved him in caring for the ill kindergartner, but he wasn't sure he had any others left in his face.

"Does Fernando know about the leak?" he continued before the secretary had a chance to reply to his first query.

"Yes," she responded coolly, having long since become accustomed to her boss's impatient, at times even brooding style — and having just gotten off the phone with the school janitor. "And," she continued, anticipating his next worry, "he's on his way to the mess in the lobby."

"Good," Rabbi Solomon was forced to admit. Then, from his office, a dozen feet away, he called out, "What about my schedule?"

Not about to strain her voice for no good reason, Cindy picked up the phone and buzzed the rabbi where he sat.

"Well, the fire marshal's your first appointment. You know, that business about the drills?"

Last year, the last week of school had arrived with the school hopelessly behind in its quota of fire drills. So Rabbi Solomon had squeezed several into the final days of the year. The kids had been quite amused but the fire department hadn't.

The rabbi moaned.

"And then the student council president has an appointment at ten," the disembodied voice pronounced, like a judge passing sentence, "about the yearbook deficit."

A strange, clearly unhappy sound emerged from the speaker on Cindy's desk.

"And between the two," she continued, "I scheduled Mr. Gomes for a half-hour. He called late yesterday to ask if he could meet with you."

"Ovadyah Gomes?" Rabbi Solomon wondered. "What about?" he asked Cindy.

"Didn't say. Uh, the fire marshal's here, Rabbi."

Rabbi Solomon instinctively began to practice his smile.

Forty minutes later, Cindy felt sorry for her boss. He'd been the fireman's captive for so long that he had likely been subjected to the full range of fire safety rules, tips and stories. She had to admit, though, that she rather enjoyed being the only one capable of rescuing him at moments like this. She cleared her throat and paused a moment.

"Rabbi," she finally spoke urgently into the intercom, "your next appointment is waiting."

"Oh thank you," came the emphatic and entirely sincere reply.

A moment later, Rabbi Solomon and his visitor emerged. Even with hat in hand, the fireman dwarfed his host.

"Thank you so much for coming by," Rabbi Solomon said, somehow summoning a broad goodbye smile and sending it up to his visitor.

The fire marshal acknowledged the rabbi's gratitude with a more modest smile and Ovadyah, who had actually only just arrived, stood up. Rabbi Solomon welcomed him into his office.

"What's the story, Mr. Gomes? I hope everything's all right with the twins' schooling." *He's probably feeling some heat from the Beth Am crowd*, he thought to himself, *and is ready to move the girls back to the Finkelstein School.*

"Everything's fine, thank God," Ovadyah reassured his host. <%0>"What I want to talk to you about has nothing to do with Hope Heights Hebrew. I just want to ask you a question."

"Certainly."

"Am I Jewish?"

Mordechai Solomon sat dumbfounded for a second or two. Then, recovering from his initial shock, he cleared his throat several times, opened and closed his desk drawer and fidgeted noticeably in his seat.

"Why do you ask?" was all he could say. When he heard how that sounded, he tried again. "I mean, what do you *mean*, are you Jewish? You're a convert, aren't you? I mean, that's what you told me, isn't it?"

"Yes, of course, but I'm a Conservative convert. Am I Jewish in *your* eyes?"

Rabbi Solomon felt a sad resignation. This was no time for evasion or public relations doublespeak. This was a sincere query from a sincere man and it deserved a sincere, clear and direct reply.

"No, I'm afraid you're not," he said quietly.

"Aha!" Ovadyah exclaimed. "I knew it!"

Taken aback by his visitor's apparent glee, the rabbi knit his brow and said simply, "Uh, I don't think I understand."

"Well," Ovadyah explained, "now I finally know for sure where I stand and what I have to do."

"You don't have to do anything," the rabbi said.

"Yes, I do," Ovadyah insisted quietly but firmly. "I have to convert."

"No, you don't."

"But I want to."

Silence.

"And I intend to."

More silence.

"Will you help me?" Ovadyah asked.

Rabbi Solomon wanted to hesitate, if only to project deliberation, but he could not. He may have only known Ovadyah for several months, but that was long enough not to doubt his sincerity.

"If you want me to," he heard himself say.

Rabbi Solomon remembered how impressed he'd been with Ovadyah back when they had discussed the twins' enrollment in the school. Now he was even more impressed. The man was not only honest, he had the courage of his convictions. He had faced the most challenging implication of all and had refused to back down.

What impressed Rabbi Solomon most, though, was something he couldn't put into words. There was something strikingly *sublime* about this Gomes fellow's demeanor, his character, his *essence*. It imbued the way he spoke, and even his body language — some nebulous but inescapable grace. The rabbi remembered that one approach to the concept of conversion in Jewish tradition considers converts truly Jewish souls that have somehow lost their identity and finally wound their way back to their spiritual source through the maze of other peoples, faiths and lands.

"Ovadyah," he continued, "do you feel ready to do all that is necessary to convert according to Halachah?"

"Yes," came the unadorned, unqualified and unhesitating answer.

"Even things you may never have thought about?"

"Whatever Judaism throws at me," Ovadyah replied.

"*Na'aseh venishma*," Rabbi Solomon thought, just like the "We will do and we will listen" the Jewish people declared at Sinai. *He is ready to accept Judaism without even knowing what it might demand of him!*

"All right," Rabbi Solomon said quietly, "the first thing we have to confront is your handicap."
"Handicap?"

"Well, we have to be realistic. You've got a double complication. First of all, you've already considered yourself Jewish on the basis of your Conservative conversion. That is no reason for anyone to be biased against you once you convert according to Halachah, of course, but some Orthodox people are probably accustomed to thinking of you as one of the 'factory converts.'"

"Tell me about it," Ovadyah mused aloud, remembering his recent experiences in Orthodox shuls. He also understood the phrase Rabbi Solomon had used all too well.

Each year, Beth Am sponsored what it called its "Make Mine Judaism!" seminar, which was essentially a series of conversion classes. Rather than identifying people who would be dedicated to Judaism, the program simply familiarized those in attendance with the Jewish social scene and the more visible rituals and taboos. Most of the participants arrived in pairs, each neophyte accompanied by a Jewish spouse or intended; the de facto purpose of the classes was undeniably to legitimate intermarriages, to help smooth over any objections the Jewish partner's parents might have. At two hundred dollars a shot ("Fee includes actual conversion, including mikvah, and all classes!" the color brochure gushed), the dozens of people who attended each year represented a welcome source of income for the synagogue, too. "Convert factory" was not, Ovadyah knew, an unreasonable description.

"The fact that you are married to a Jew," Rabbi Solomon continued, "will only strengthen this impression, unfortunately."

The rabbi paused for a long moment.

"And looking like a Yemenite when everyone knows you're not isn't going to help you, either. Let's face it: to your average, snow-white American, you're black."

Ovadyah was not black — his complexion reflected one of the many hues of the Cape Verde Islands — but he knew how easily European-stock Americans lumped dark people together. Rabbi Solomon was probably right, he thought.

Ovadyah himself had little tolerance for the popular image of the American black; the impoverished Eastern European shtetl-dweller was closer to his idea of a real person than the stereotypical American ghetto brother with a boom-box growing like some grotesque tumor from his shoulder. He knew how futile it was to try to convince people who seldom mixed with blacks that that element was atypical of black society; statistics were no match for visibility. And he knew how grossly insensitive the average middle-class white person was to the realities of black poverty. He wondered if the Jewish middle class might even be more intolerant as a result of its own collective Horatio Alger story in America.

"Even if it's as bad as you say," Ovadyah continued, "it's bound to be better than some of the sham acceptance I've experienced until now. I was fawned over like a newborn baby at Beth Am at times, but I eventually learned to tell which smiles were for real. I think I'd almost welcome whatever confrontation would be necessary to become truly and totally accepted by other Jews."
"There needn't be any confrontation," Rabbi Solomon interjected. "Once it's known that you have properly converted and that your commitment to Judaism is real, your skin color will be as meaningless as your eye color to the Orthodox who know you as a *ger*, a true convert. They'll think of you as a Jew, no more and no less. All I meant was that, unless the conversion is done with the utmost care and according to the highest standards, your ethnic background might make it hard for some to accept its validity."

"I understand. So what do you think is necessary?"

"Well, first of all, we are not going to handle this locally. Hope Heights isn't exactly a major Orthodox community. To assure that the conversion will be beyond reproach, it must be performed under the guidance of world-class rabbis. We'll have to go to New York."

"No problem."

"Was your wife ever married before?" Rabbi Solomon asked, witching tracks without warning.

"Uh...why, yes, as a matter of fact, she was," Ovadyah answered slowly, wondering where the question had come from.

The rabbi's heart sank.

"Divorced?" he asked further, trying to conceal his mounting concern.

"Yes," came the reply. "Is that a problem?"

"Well, it could be. Was her first husband Jewish?"

"Yes, I believe he was."

Another grimace.

"Do you know if she received a Jewish divorce from him?"

"I'm not sure. I'll have to check."

Rabbi Solomon took a deep breath before he spoke.

"If a Jewish woman was legally — from the standpoint of Halachah, that is — married to a Jewish man but never halachically divorced from him, any subsequent marriage she entered into would not have the status of a marriage at all, but would be considered an adulterous union — as she would still be technically married to her original husband according to Jewish law. Any children born later would be considered *mamzerim*," he explained.

"Bastards?" Ovadyah asked, remembering the word "mamzer" from somewhere or other.

"Well, not in the English sense. Essentially, a *mamzer* may only marry another *mamzer* — *mamzeres* is the female term — or a convert. It can be quite a difficult situation."

Ovadyah felt his heart in his throat.

"If my wife didn't receive a Jewish divorce, would that make the twins *mamzerim* — uh, *mamzeros*?"

Rabbi Solomon thought a moment and then the look of pain that had crept across his face moments before suddenly faded.

"Fortunately, I don't think so. Only if their father was Jewish at the time of their conception, which you were not."

Ovadyah heaved a sigh of relief.

"We'll have to confirm that with a halachic authority, of course," Rabbi Solomon continued, "but I'm pretty sure there's no problem there. However, if a Jewish divorce was never secured for your wife, she would immediately be off-limits to you — since she'd still be married to someone else — until we locate her former husband and convince him to go through the divorce procedure."

"Wow." That was all Ovadyah could muster in response as he pictured the fellow receiving that bolt from out of the blue.

"In addition, if there was no Jewish divorce and we have to arrange one, we would need a separation period afterward."

"Separation?" Ovadyah asked quizzically.

"Between you and your wife. So that any pregnancy that occurs after the conversion can be assured to have resulted from your marriage, not from that of your wife and her previous husband."

Ovadyah's quizzical look intensified.

"But she hasn't seen him in fifteen years!" he protested.

"The Halachah," Rabbi Solomon explained gently, "insists on a separation period."

"But just for enough time to ascertain that there was no pregnancy at the time of divorce, right?"

"You got it. Three months."

"Three months?" Ovadyah's incredulity spilled across the rabbi's desk.

"Yes, I'm afraid," Rabbi Solomon replied. "The Halachah considers only visible changes in a woman's body to be evidence of pregnancy, and these are believed to take three months to appear."

"Ah," said Ovadyah, "but what if no pregnancy is possible? My wife is not capable of conceiving."

Ovadyah took the silence as his cue to elaborate.

"After the twins were born, Ariella and I decided not to have more children, so she had a tubal ligation."

"I see," Rabbi Solomon said pensively, "but unfortunately, I don't think that carries any halachic weight. The separation period will still probably be necessary if no halachic divorce was arranged when your wife's first marriage ended. But I'll check into it anyway."

Rabbi Solomon wondered if the separation requirement might be too much for Ovadyah to handle, as his guest suddenly seemed absorbed in his thoughts. Yet Ovadyah was only concerned with learning the details of the separation and planning its logistics. His acceptance of the requirement was never an issue. He had accepted Judaism; there was nothing else to say.

Rabbi Solomon watched Ovadyah's face go through varied perturbations: lips tightening, brow furrowing and eyebrows rising and falling. He imagined his guest agonizing over whether conversion was really worth the trouble, fearing future demands Judaism might make on him, doubting the religion's very validity. Ovadyah, though, was simply working out the details of the separation, deciding how to explain things to the kids, and anticipating Ariella's reaction.

"No problem," he said quickly when he had finished formulating a basic battle plan.

Rabbi Solomon was taken aback by the starkness of this answer. "Are you sure?" he asked. He needed to be perfectly certain that Ovadyah's dedication to Jewish law was total and unwavering. "Of course," Ovadyah said simply, "If that's what it takes, I'll do it."

Rabbi Solomon repressed a broad, joyous smile. He didn't want his reaction to play any role in Ovadyah's decision to follow through with things. To think, he told himself, that he had been sure he'd run out of smiles hours ago.

"So," Rabbi Solomon concluded, "I guess you and your wife have a lot to talk about."

They certainly did, and later that evening, as the twins sat in the adjoining room doing their homework, Ovadyah began to recount the details of his conversation with Rabbi Solomon to Ariella. She listened attentively as her husband told her about the need for a halachic divorce from her previous husband, and about the separation that would be required if such a divorce was never granted.

"It's all right," she said. "I got a *get*."

"Say what?"

"I got a *get*," she repeated, "A *get*. A Jewish divorce. I only remember the word because I thought it nicely expressed each spouse's message to the other: `*Get* outta my life.' It's Hebrew, of course, and it just means `document' — I think that's what the rabbi told me back then. I was really surprised that Bob had arranged for a religious divorce altogether. I guess the rabbi had insisted on it."

"Good for him," Ovadyah said. "Had he neglected the *get* and had you then married a Jewish man instead of me, your children would have been *mamzerim*."

"Show-off," Ariella sneered. "Just because I knew what a *get* was and you didn't, you have to prove you know more Hebrew than I do, don't you? All right, what're *mamzerim*?"

"Products of a forbidden union," Ovadyah explained, "like an adulterous one."

He went on to describe the import of being a *mamzer* and why the lack of a *get* was so serious. Ariella was rapt.

"You mean if a rabbi marries a couple without researching the bride's history, or officiates at a divorce where the *get* isn't up to snuff, he's practically producing *mamzerim*?"

"I suppose so," Ovadyah said, thinking just what his wife was thinking, that there were probably thousands of Conservative and Reform Jews who had been — or would be — married by rabbis entirely unconcerned with such details of Jewish law, resulting in myriad persistent and grave halachic problems. Eating non-kosher food or violating the Sabbath laws seemed almost minor issues by comparison.

Thankful that their own situation probably would not suffer from anyone's nonchalance about Jewish law, they moved upstairs, where Ariella thought the *get* probably lay stashed amid her old papers and things.

Several hours later, the distant past lay strewn piecemeal all around the room. But no *get*.

"I don't get it," she muttered.

"Dear," Ovadyah said with a smile that belied his nervousness, "this is no time for punning."

"Very funny," Ariella acknowledged the joke, her own nervousness less concealed, "but I really can't imagine where it could be. Could I have thrown it out? It's possible, I suppose. I certainly didn't think of it as anything very important at the time."

"Well," Ovadyah sighed, "I guess Bob's going to get an unexpected visit from bygone days very soon."

"And I guess it's time we separate," Ariella reminded her erstwhile husband.

"Hey, not so fast. If you're sure you got a *get*, maybe that's enough."

"Call Rabbi Solomon," Ariella suggested.

He did. All Ariella heard from Ovadyah's end of the conversation were "uh-huh"s. When he hung up the phone, though, she saw in his expression what the answer had been.

"Well," he began, "he felt that since we don't know if the *get* — even *if* it exists — is halachically valid, we couldn't rely on it. He told me he'd try to track down your ex tomorrow and find out who the officiating rabbi was and if there is some record of the divorce.

"What if the get turns out to have been invalid?" he asked. "You think we'll be able to handle three months of singlehood?"

"We'll have to manage somehow," she replied without hesitation.

"You're great," he said, and meant it.

Ariella ignored the compliment. She had become just as serious about Judaism as her husband, and, like him, did not consider the requirements of Jewish law to be subject to anyone's personal approval.

"Did you tell him we can't have any more children?" she asked suddenly.

Over the past several months, Ariella had grown increasingly sensitive to the import of the decision she had made so long ago. A decade earlier, she and Ovadyah had been young professionals with as many children as they could ever imagine caring for. A permanent solution to the perpetual threat of pregnancy had seemed, at the time, ideal.

Of late, though, she had come to reconsider her decision. Maybe it was the proverbial biological tick-tock driving her subconscious mad, she told herself. But one thing she knew was exactly when her queasy regret had set in.

She and Ovadyah had been at services at Beth Am — it couldn't have been more than a year or two earlier — and the junior rabbi, whose main role at the synagogue was teaching Israeli dancing in the adult education program, was delivering the sermon. His topic was the importance of large Jewish families.

As he reminded the congregation of the loss of millions of Jews during the Holocaust, Ariella thought of her own parents, the only survivors of their respective families. As the rabbi sadly noted how so many Jewish couples were barely replacing themselves within the Jewish people, having only one or two children, she thought of herself. And as he spoke about children, their beauty, their importance, their meaning for the Jewish future, she found herself hurting.

As weeks and then months went by, the sermon's words seemed to knock at her heart, demanding admission. She had shared her ache with Ovadyah and he had sympathized, but what could he do? Ariella had even broached the subject with her doctor, but he had dismissed any attempt to reverse the operation as irrational, unlikely to succeed and entirely unnecessary.

"You've got two beautiful children," he had told her in exasperation. "Why torture yourself with operations, tests and pregnancies now?"

While the desire for a larger family still incubated deep in the warmth of her soul, Ariella had forced herself to accept, at least outwardly, the doctor's sentiments. Now, though, the thought of Ovadyah's conversation with Rabbi Solomon had stirred her feelings again.

"Well, yes," Ovadyah replied, "I did bring it up in passing to see if it might make the separation period unnecessary."

An odd, brooding silence ensued, until Ovadyah broke it.

"You all right?"

"Fine," Ariella answered.

But Ovadyah was not convinced. Neither, for that matter, was Ariella.

CHAPTER 19

Sage Counsel

Rabbi Evyon tried to hide his nervousness as he began class with an announcement.

"Guys," he announced, loudly banging his hand on his desk to quiet the small group of boisterous high school boys, "we have a really special opportunity today."

The boys grew suddenly silent but their faces showed more cynicism than excitement. A "special opportunity," they knew well, could easily spell trouble. The nine fifteen-year-olds waited to hear if the announcement merited a round of moans (anything making demands on their free time) or applause (anything affording them a bit more of it).

In a friendly tone just serious enough to keep his students from either response, the bearded, thirtyish Talmud teacher revealed, "I just found out that we're having a special guest sit in on *shiur* today. A *very* special guest."

"Special guest?" one cynic ventured. "Not the Feds again, I hope."

There was pointedly little enthusiasm in the boy's pungent reference to the semi-yearly visit of the local Jewish Federation representative, on which substantial school funding hinged.

"No," Rabbi Evyon said with a smile. "This is an entirely different kind of visitor. As a matter of fact, he's one of this generation's great *talmidei chachamim*."

After a moment of puzzled silence, one of the boys said what all his classmates had been thinking.

"C'mon, really?"

Hope Heights, after all, was hardly a major stopover for renowned Torah scholars.

"I kid you not," Rabbi Evyon replied, jumping to his feet and leaning forward across his desk at his students. "And I'm talking major *rosh yeshivah* here. *Gadol* city," he deadpanned, using the Hebrew term for a world-class Jewish leader.

Rabbi Evyon paused to let the suspense build before letting the other shoe drop.

"The rosh yeshivah of Chaim Berlin," he said finally, "Rav Aharon Schechter."

Several eyebrows shot up at the mention of one of the most celebrated yeshivos and its venerable dean.

"He's coming *here*? To *our shiur*?" one asked incredulously.

Those less familiar with the yeshivah world whispered questions to their neighbors and seemed suitably impressed upon receiving their replies.

Rabbi Evyon explained that Rabbi Solomon had invited the esteemed scholar to visit the yeshivah and suggest ways of strengthening it. Then, satisfied that everyone had grasped the full import of the occasion, Rabbi Evyon began his lesson. The boys seemed unusually attentive, he noted, correctly surmising that no one wanted to be a space cadet in the presence of a *gadol*.

A half-hour or so later, the door opened and Rabbi Solomon poked his cherubic countenance into the room. After verifying that none of the students was hanging from a light fixture or arm-wrestling Rabbi Evyon — situations he had come across on other visits to the room — he opened the door wider to let himself and his guest in.

At the sight of the jet-black coat and snow-white beard of the older man ushered in by Rabbi Solomon, the students and their rebbe immediately rose reverently from their seats.

The visitor seemed embarrassed to have interrupted the class but a broad smile spread across his strikingly handsome face as soon as he sat in the chair offered him. Did he always *glow* like that, one of the boys wondered.

Rabbi Evyon tried to squelch his apprehension at having to "say a *shiur*" in the presence of a celebrated scholar like Rabbi Schechter. At least, he reassured himself, he had prepared an especially elaborate lesson late the previous night, when he had been notified of the *rosh yeshivah*'s visit, a *shiur* designed to demonstrate his students' abilities — and his own — to the fullest.

And so the rebbe launched into the next portion of his discourse, constructing an impressively logical edifice on an oddly worded comment by Rashi, the premier medieval Talmudic commentary. He went on for nearly an hour, much of the time occupied by his students' questions and arguments. All in all, it went just as he'd hoped. He found himself musing wishfully about how much easier his job would be were a renowned rabbi present in his classroom throughout the school year; it had been a good day.

When the *shiur* was over and the boys filed out of the room, Rabbi Schechter shook hands with each of them and then with Rabbi Evyon.

"Your *shiur* was excellent!" he enthused as the younger man blushed. "I was truly impressed, especially by the participation of your *talmidim*."

Rabbi Evyon couldn't wait to tell his students that the *rosh yeshivah* had complimented them. Then Rabbi Schechter guided him away from where Rabbi Solomon stood talking to one of the boys, and sat down with him at a student's desk.

"That Rashi, though," he said quietly but excitedly, opening the nearest tome, "look at it again."

Rabbi Evyon looked down at the text — and then up at the radiant face within the corona of white hair and beard. Rabbi Schechter pointed down at the space between two words.

"Imagine two dots right here," he said.

"What?" Rabbi Evyon asked in bewilderment.

"Well, it doesn't happen very often, but sometimes the copyist or printer messes up," the venerable sage said with a little laugh, "and the two dots used to indicate the end of a comment are left out by accident. Picture two dots right here."

Rabbi Evyon looked where Rabbi Schechter was pointing and a sudden realization descended with all the subtlety of an avalanche. He had misread Rashi's comment! His entire lecture had been based on a misprint. His impressive edifice had been built on quicksand.

"Of course" was all Rabbi Evyon could muster.

Rabbi Schechter squeezed his new protégé's shoulder warmly and somehow managed to increase the wattage of his powerful smile.

Meanwhile, Rabbi Solomon had approached from across the room.

"If it's all right with the *rosh yeshivah*," he spoke to his guest in the third person, as observant Jews customarily do when addressing a very learned person, "I'd like to introduce him to the gentleman I spoke about earlier."

"Certainly!" came the eager reply and Rabbi Schechter sprang to his feet.

Rabbi Evyon followed suit and the older man thanked him for the opportunity to sit in his *shiur*. The high school rebbe felt an odd sadness at his venerable guest's departure. Though his next class was only a few minutes away, Rabbi Evyon instinctively tagged along with the other two rabbis as they started down the hall to a private office. Outside the office door, someone was waiting to meet with them. Rabbi Solomon introduced the fellow to the visiting sage, unlocked the office door and ushered the other two men in.

As Rabbi Evyon watched the door close, he bid the *rosh yeshivah* a silent goodbye. Though they had only just met, he felt oddly attached to him.

Jogging down the hall to his next class, however, he couldn't help but wonder what business the celebrated Rav Aharon Schechter could possibly have with some *shvartze*.

CHAPTER 20

New York

R abbi Solomon glanced at the speedometer and instinctively eased off the accelerator just in time to see the telltale antenna of an unmarked patrol car. He seemed to have a sixth sense about such things.

"Just outside of New York, they're thick as flies around a carcass," he said.

"Interesting metaphor," remarked Ovadyah from the back seat, where he sat with his wife, who chuckled her agreement. Neither of them had ever cared for New York, even when they'd lived there. Sure, it was an *interesting* place, but it was also corrupt, crumbling, squalid and downright frightening at times. It wasn't really even a nice place to visit.

"Oh, I don't know," Rabbi Solomon replied. "I enjoy being in the city, even if the ride in is usually a pain. There's so much to do here."

"I can't exactly picture you at the Museum of Modern Art, Rabbi, or taking in an opera," Ariella admitted.

"Nah, not that kind of stuff," the rabbi said. "I mean the Jewish stuff: the bookstores, the clothing stores — "

"Clothing stores?" Ariella asked.

"Well, you know, *Jewish* clothing, the kinds of things you can't find so easily in Feldstein's," Rabbi Solomon explained, referring to Hope Heights' premier department store. "Things like black, felt hats, or summer dresses with sleeves, or tzitzis or *tichels* — "

"Kichels?" Ovadyah queried incredulously, recalling the hard, hollow, cookie-like affairs some of the older men liked to crunch on with a shot of whiskey after morning services at Beth Am's "upstairs minyan." "Doesn't the Jewish bakery at home carry them?" he asked.

"*Tichels*, not *kichels*," the rabbi said with a hearty laugh. "You know, those kerchiefs Orthodox women use to cover their hair."

As Ovadyah committed the new word to memory, Ariella winced at the thought of women forced to hide their hair. She knew that Dina Rosen and the other frum women in Hope Heights always wore either a *tichel* or a wig, even in their own homes. She had always assumed that the practice was just a voluntary convention within the Orthodox community, but she'd recently read that it was an actual law in Judaism, a standard of modesty that, she had to admit, she had a hard time relating to. As she pondered the prospect of sacrificing her hair to a new lifestyle, her thoughts were interrupted by Rabbi Solomon's voice. New York's Jewish pleasures had evoked a certain exuberance in the man.

"But most of all, the restaurants!" the rabbi gushed. "There are kosher French, kosher Italian and even kosher Chinese eateries — not to mention kosher fast-food places!"

Ovadyah and Ariella had indeed found, since they had adopted the Jewish dietary laws, that they missed being able to eat out, and to eat whatever they wanted whenever they wanted. They had been keeping kosher for many months now and, since the Chowder Pot debacle, had not eaten in a single restaurant. Still, they couldn't quite capture Rabbi Solomon's enthusiasm at the dining prospects in the big city.

"But of course," the rabbi continued, returning from his flight of fancy to culinary heaven, "we're not going to New York to eat, now are we?"

"Well, no," said Ovadyah, pausing ever so slightly for effect, "but after we meet with Rabbi Rabinowitz, there's no reason not to take in a little something before we head back, is there?"

His words had the desired effect and Rabbi Solomon happily resumed his former speed, though not for long, due to traffic congestion and construction work on the road.

The last twenty miles of the trip into Boro Park, the Brooklyn mecca of East Coast Orthodox Jewry, took nearly an hour, and by the time they arrived in the community's heart, Ovadyah and Ariella were staring out their respective windows, wide-eyed as children at a drive-through zoo. "Wow!" was all Ariella could say. Ovadyah was silent but his eyes and smile concurred.

Neither of them had ever seen so many Jews in one place, at least never so many Jewish-looking Jews. Women in below-kneelength, long-sleeved dresses strode down the sidewalk of the busy business district pushing baby carriages, their older children beside them. And men sported sidelocks and beards, many dressed in dark suits or long, black caftans and black, felt hats. Others wore shirtsleeves and knit yarmulkes. Some carried books, others briefcases or shopping bags, but none could have looked any more Jewish had Stars of David been stamped on their foreheads.

The Gomeses had seen such people before, of course, both when they'd lived in Manhattan and even in Hope Heights, but never *so many in one place*. They were taken aback at the sheer number of people that filled their field of view.

"Welcome to 13th Avenue," Rabbi Solomon said, noticing his passengers' rapture. "I thought we might cruise down the strip a bit before going to Rabbi Rabinowitz's shul — it's just two minutes from here."

He received no argument.

When they had driven a few more blocks, past a Chassidic boys' school that had just released a veritable sea of sidelocks, and then past a few poorly dressed, elderly women soliciting charity from passersby, they turned off the main street and, several turns later, arrived at their destination.

Rabbi Solomon had long known of Rabbi Rabinowitz's reputation as a trusted overseer of conversions. Not only was he meticulous in his adherence to Jewish law, but he had an uncanny ability to discern ulterior motives or dishonesty on the part of aspiring converts.

A tall, stately gentleman with a neat, black beard, Rabbi Rabinowitz rose from behind a desk as they entered his study. He shook hands with the men and bowed slightly with a warm smile to Ariella. Knowing well by that point that Orthodox men avoid physical contact with women other than their wives, she suppressed the reflex to extend her hand.

"Please sit down," the rabbi said, motioning toward a small couch against one wall. He moved his chair from behind the desk over to the couch and everyone got comfortable.

"It is a pleasure to meet you, Mr. and Mrs. Gomes. Rabbi Solomon has told me a lot about you, all of it quite impressive."

"And true," Rabbi Solomon interjected as the couple blushed. "Rav Aharon Schechter suggested we contact you regarding conversion."

"Well, there is a *beis din* here in Brooklyn," the other rabbi explained, using the Hebrew term for a Jewish court, "with which I work on conversion cases, but things sometimes move somewhat slowly in issues like these. By necessity, of course."

Ovadyah's face registered almost imperceptible disappointment. He had hardly expected to proceed directly to the *mikvah*, but the rabbi's cautionary words seemed to bode a long delay. He didn't want to wait any more than absolutely necessary.

"Why don't we begin," Rabbi Rabinowitz continued, "with a few questions?"

After inquiring about Ovadyah's first interest in Judaism, his understanding of Jewish law and life and the Jewish lifestyle he had already adopted, the rabbi asked him to list some books he'd read about Judaism.

There were so many, and he had gleaned so much knowledge from *people*, that Ovadyah felt strangely at a loss. He finally recalled two books he had read several years earlier, at the very

131

start of his quest; their titles had most likely materialized in his mind because back then, he had carried them on a piece of paper for several weeks, looking at them a few times each day before finding the courage to actually enter a Jewish bookstore and buy them.

"Uh, well, there was *To Be A Jew*, for one," he finally said.

Rabbi Rabinowitz nodded his familiarity with the book. He had a few problems with parts of it but, all in all, it wasn't a bad introduction to Judaism.

Ovadyah was happy to see the rabbi's nod and happier still to feel the other title, which had eluded him until just then, come rolling off his tongue. It was the book Rabbi Shoman had considered too Orthodox back when Ovadyah had put it on the reading list for Beth Am's adult education program. He certainly hadn't studied it since then, but at least he had its name.

"And *A Guide for the Jewish Homemaker*," he said almost triumphantly.

Rabbi Rabinowitz hesitated a moment, one of his eyebrows leaped skyward and he coughed softly in embarrassment.

Rabbi Solomon winced and turned a red that nicely matched his beard.

Ovadyah and Ariella were amused at first at how the older rabbi's eyebrows seemed to lead separate lives, but they quickly realized something was amiss. Neither, however, understood just how inopportune it had been to mention that particular bestseller. Its author, Rose Blumenthal, a self-styled "Orthodox feminist," held some decidedly unorthodox opinions. Hardly the ideal role model for a potential convert, for someone expected — like the Jewish people at Sinai — to accept the laws and demands of Judaism wholeheartedly and *in toto*. And decidedly *not* the ideal reference to name in Rabbi Rabinowitz's study.

Bobbing up and down in his seat like a red buoy, Rabbi Solomon endeavored to save the ship in distress.

"Uh, Rabbi Rabinowitz," he began, "Ovadyah has amassed much information from *many* sources — from *frum* families, discussions with rabbis and much other learning he has done from original sources."

"Yes," Rabbi Rabinowitz said with affected reassurance, "I'm sure he has. I just want to get a handle on precisely what areas of Jewish law he and Mrs. Gomes have covered so that I can ascertain that they are aware of some of the more taxing demands of Halachah."

Then, his raised eyebrow finally rejoining its companion, the rabbi turned to Ovadyah and asked, "What areas are you presently studying?"

"Well," came the quiet, confident reply, "I've been learning the *Kitzur* with Rabbi Solomon, at Rabbi Schechter's suggestion, and the siddur as well."

Ovadyah pronounced the name of the popular condensation of Jewish laws pertinent to daily life and the Hebrew word for the prayer book as if he had been using both often, which indeed he had.

Rabbi Rabinowitz smiled and seemed more at ease again.

"Mr. and Mrs. Gomes," he said after a moment's thought, "would you allow Rabbi Solomon and me to confer for a few minutes?"

"Certainly," Ovadyah replied for both of them.

"Let me show you where the shul library is. We have a good many books in English you might enjoy browsing through a bit...."

When the rabbi reentered his study, Rabbi Solomon rose and began to explain Ovadyah's reference to the Blumenthal book, but Rabbi Rabinowitz dismissed his visitor's efforts with a wave of his hand and a smile.

"That doesn't mean anything to me, really. It's perfectly understandable that he would come across books like that at one point or another. Tell me, though, how is he when you learn with him? Is he sincere? What sort of questions does he ask? Is he faithful to the study schedule?"

Rabbi Solomon was happy to hear the questions; they had easy answers.

"Rabbi Rabinowitz, I can't tell you what a pleasure it is learning with Ovadyah. Not only is he always on time, he lets me have it, in his gentle way, if I'm late! And he gobbles up everything eagerly. He's like a child in a way. Not intellectually — he's very sharp — but in his openness, his refusal to assume airs or hide behind 'sophistication.' He comprehends everything well and is very observance-oriented."

"By which you mean?"

"He sees everything we learn in terms of how to shoulder his responsibilities as a Jew. He learns in order to know what to do."

"Well, that's certainly encouraging. I have to tell you, I do have a good feeling about him, even from the short time you've been here. Tell me, where is she holding?"

"His wife? She's squarely behind him," Rabbi Solomon replied.

He had been greatly impressed with Ariella's spiritual growth over the months he'd gotten to know her and her husband. She was certainly not the type to blindly go wherever her husband led; she had a mind of her own and wasn't afraid to voice her thoughts and opinions. But Ariella was strong, not stubborn. If adopting Judaism made sense, then that is what she would do. Rabbi Solomon had no doubt that that was where she was heading. She had stood by Ovadyah in his choices, and had as little patience with wishy-washiness as he did. Her husband's determination may have irritated her initially but it had become a catalyst for examining who she was, and a challenge to her complacent acceptance of Jewishness as nothing more than an ethnic identity. "Any complications with regard to her status?"

"Well," Rabbi Solomon hesitated a moment but then realized there was really no reason to hedge, "just her previous marriage."

"To a Jew?" Rabbi Rabinowitz asked apprehensively.

"Yes, and there was supposedly a *get*, though she never could find it. The previous husband was contacted but it wasn't clear who presided over the giving of the *get*."

"And was a new *get* arranged?"

"Yes," Rabbi Solomon assured his questioner. "She should receive it within the week. We had a rabbi in the ex-husband's city arrange for the writing and delivery."

Rabbi Rabinowitz knew there would be considerable expense involved in the writing of the *get* — it needed the skills of an experienced scribe — and in its hand-delivery to Ariella. He also believed very strongly that any man or woman endeavoring to fulfill the requirements of the Torah should not have to bear the financial burden. As a matter of fact, he administered a fund whose resources were intended for precisely such situations.

"Will the costs be covered?" he asked, ready to offer whatever assistance might be needed.

"*Baruch Hashem*," Rabbi Solomon assured him, "I had no trouble raising the funds. A few people in Hope Heights were more than ready to help."

"That's wonderful," Rabbi Rabinowitz said with pensive satisfaction. "And of course, since the father isn't Jewish, there's no problem of *mamzerus* with his children."

"Nonetheless," Rabbi Solomon interjected, "Ovadyah didn't want anyone to ever question his daughters' status, so he insisted that I confirm the matter beyond a shadow of a doubt. So I contacted Reb Moshe."

"You got through to Reb Moshe? When?"

"Just last week. The call back came only yesterday."

Rabbi Solomon understood his host's surprise well. Reb Moshe Feinstein, the most respected Orthodox scholar and leader of the generation, was widely known to be deathly ill, and it hadn't been easy to convince the great sage's secretary, a respected rabbi in his own right, to put the question of the twins' status to the ailing scholar. But Ovadyah had been determined to establish his family's standing beyond any question. So, through the miracles of human persistence and automatic dialing, Rabbi Solomon had succeeded in reaching Reb Moshe. When the answer finally came, Ovadyah had felt an immense weight lifted from his heart.

A particularly painful jolt would shake the Orthodox world several weeks later at the news of Reb Moshe's death. But Ovadyah would take special comfort in the knowledge that the great leader's legacy had included his decision regarding the Gomes children, which turned out to be one of the last of his life.

"Well," Rabbi Rabinowitz continued, "I think we should call our friends back in now and set a target date for the *geirus*. I assume Ovadyah is familiar with the procedure."

"Yes. This will be his second *hatafah*."

Rabbi Rabinowitz felt both regret at the need for Ovadyah to undergo the circumcision ceremony again and admiration for the convert's commitment.

"I don't see any need to wait the several months I usually insist on to ascertain the candidate's stability. Both your experience with him and my gut feeling speak for an accelerated schedule. Do make sure, though," he added after a moment, "that you cover the pertinent Shabbos laws with both him and his wife as soon as possible. They are the most important and complex ones for them to learn well before the *geirus*."

Rabbi Solomon nodded in assurance and the two men ascended the stairs to the library. When they entered, they found Ariella halfway up a small ladder, putting a book back on a shelf, and Ovadyah seated at a table in a corner, softly rocking back and forth before a large, open tome, quietly reading the words aloud. It was a volume of the Talmud with English translation. The rabbis approached him and he looked up, startled.

"Already?" he asked with a sudden, sincere smile. "I was just getting into it."

"Listen, Ovadyah," Rabbi Solomon said with mock sternness, "I told you we'd start learning *Gemara* right after the *geirus*. Must you always rush ahead with things?"

Ovadyah grinned. He remembered how he and Rabbi Solomon had learned several weeks earlier that the desire to undertake more than what is reasonably possible is a fundamental Jewish characteristic, as evidenced at Sinai when the Jewish people said, "We will do" before "We will hear." They had also studied a Talmudic narrative describing the Jews, in the same vein, as a "hasty people."

Both rabbis thought of the same passage as they smiled back at Ovadyah.

After afternoon prayers in the shul, the rabbis and the Gomeses returned to Rabbi Rabinowitz's study to finalize arrangements and bid their farewells. When the date for the actual *geirus* was set for two weeks later, Ovadyah breathed a sigh of relief, chiding himself for having feared a major delay.

The threesome thanked the Brooklyn rabbi warmly for arranging the conversion. Then they set out for a walk through Boro Park before dinner. Having often spoken about the crucial nature of Jewish learning, Rabbi Solomon and the couple gravitated to several of the Jewish bookstores that peppered the area, making a purchase or two in each.

The steady stream of unmistakably observant Jews that carried them down the streets still astonished both Ariella and Ovadyah. Many of the conversations they drifted in and out of as they walked past pedestrians were in Yiddish, a language the couple had always assumed had been consumed along with Eastern European Jewry in the Holocaust. Ariella recalled her parents speaking Yiddish at home but she'd still thought of the tongue as an atrophied part of Jewish culture. Here, though, in Boro Park, it was undeniably alive and kicking, in all its colorful, explosive expressiveness.

As the sun began to set, Rabbi Solomon led the Gomeses to a crowded, cafeteria-style fast-food establishment. Ovadyah and Ariella were amused at the sight of the large eatery.

"Goodness!" Ariella exclaimed. "It's just like a treif joint!"

"Ummgnn!" Ovadyah remarked minutes later as he chewed his first bite of hamburger. "It's just as greasy as a *treif* joint, too!"

"Hey," Rabbi Solomon said with feigned modesty, "only the best for my guests!"

"Oh, cut it out," Ariella interjected, trying her hardest to enjoy her chicken sandwich. "It's not so bad."

"Not yet, anyway," cautioned Ovadyah, a veteran of many a fast-food establishment. "Give it a few hours."

As they ate, the conversation turned to their surroundings.

"So, folks," Rabbi Solomon said, "how do you like Boro Park?"

"Fascinating," Ariella responded. "It's almost like another world. Sort of a `Planet of the Jews'!"

"I really didn't realize," Ovadyah said, "that there were so many *frum* Jews in all of America, much less in one place. But you know what really puzzles me?" he added, perplexed. "Not one of the women we saw on the streets covered her hair! Aside from a few ladies with kerchiefs, they all seemed to have just come from the hairdressers."

Ariella and Rabbi Solomon both looked at him with peculiar smiles.

"I mean," he tried again, "Jewish law requires married women to cover their hair, doesn't it?"

Silence from across the table. Just the peculiar smiles.

"I mean, they *had* to be married women — most of them were pushing baby carriages!"

The weird smiles across the table seemed to be holding yet broader ones back.

"What's the matter?" Ovadyah demanded, entirely bewildered.

"Should I tell him or do you want to?" the rabbi asked Ariella.

"I think I'd like to," Ariella replied. "Ovadyah, dear," she continued, addressing her spouse, "you didn't see one woman out there today who *wasn't* covering her hair. They were all wearing wigs."

Ovadyah could only say, "They were?" and then join in the others' laughter. How was he supposed to know, he wondered, that they made such natural-looking wigs these days?

CHAPTER 21

Future Concerns

The headiness of the trip to New York buoyed Ovadyah for days before events suddenly forced it to give way to a very different sort of feeling.

He had known for several weeks that his company was changing hands. But nothing prepared him for what ensued on his return, or for the irony it bore.

The new bosses at work were making personnel changes, and Ovadyah began to make out an intriguing pattern in the blizzard of pink slips. Incredulous, he realized that *Jews* were being summarily purged from the company.

Conspicuous even among the other Jews in the office due to his skullcap and his Sabbath observance — he would leave the office an hour or two before the official end of the workday on winter Fridays, when the Sabbath began early — Ovadyah knew that if his theory were right, he'd likely be laid off quite quickly himself.

And he was.

The irony — a bittersweet smile came to his lips when he pondered it — was that he was now the victim of anti-Semitic bias. His beliefs, not his skin tone, had branded him. There was subtle but unmistakable meaning there. Though his conversion was still a week off, he had, he mused with wry resignation, arrived.

Ovadyah's alarm clock paged him in the middle of an uneasy dream early the morning after his termination had taken effect. The buzzing flushed a torrent of discomfort from the back of his mind to the forefront of his consciousness.

He banged the clock into silent submission, stumbled into the bathroom to perform the ritual morning handwashing, and then went to the window to see if the previous day's spring-like weather had indeed been followed by the threatened drastic drop in temperature. Raising the shade, he squinted at the sudden, rude brightness, the smooth, white shroud that silently mocked him, obscuring all but the houses.

A half-hour later, Ovadyah was clearing snow from his car windshield, with only an occasional wistful look at the home he and Ariella had bought the previous year. It had been their dream house, and the sizable mortgage it necessitated had left them in well over their heads. Back then, they had counted on expected but unhatched chickens, raises that seemed all but inevitable. Now, though, Ovadyah mused, there was — at least in his case — nothing left to raise.

He got into the car and, after several tries, managed to awaken the engine. Shifting into gear, he forced the machine through the snow — and forced himself to face the likelihood of the house being relegated once more to the realm of his and Ariella's dreams.

Arriving at the synagogue a bit later than usual, Ovadyah realized he'd have to forgo his usual study period before services. He always liked to review part of the upcoming Sabbath's Torah reading in the calm quiet before services. Today, though, he barely had time to put on his tefillin. He forced his thoughts to the parchment inside the box, which displayed, among other verses, the quintessential Jewish credo, "Hear O Israel, the Lord is our God, the Lord is One." Concentration eluded him, however. Images of the future kept intruding, and aside from his impending conversion and return to Ariella, they all seemed bleak. Looking for a new job...making ends meet in the meanwhile...selling the house...finding an apartment... One thought after another stabbed at his mind. Should he file a religious discrimination complaint? Ask Rabbi Solomon why, just as he was finally about to become authentically Jewish, God was treating him so shabbily? Scream in rage? Any of those things might make him feel a little better, he reflected, but none was a *real* response, a truly *Jewish* response.

Ovadyah took the other phylactery from its embroidered pouch and placed it on his head, making the second blessing before straightening the straps above his ears and setting the knot at the precise point where his skull met his neck. Then, he surveyed the room and counted the men. He smiled a wry smile and sighed at the next trial he'd have to face that morning.

It was already two minutes after seven o'clock — when services were supposed to begin — and there were ten men present: the rabbi, eight mostly older gentlemen and Ovadyah, who knew that the rabbi would shortly start working the phones in an effort to rouse some "reservist" from his morning slumber into the inclement weather in order to "make a minyan."

Ovadyah had long since resigned himself to the fact that, until his conversion, he could not be counted as part of the quorum. Though he had been living a thoroughly Jewish life for many months, he was still, he reminded himself at times like these, a goy. I'm truly a "practicing Jew," he would joke to himself — only practicing, not yet really part of Judaism.

At least that day, Ovadyah consoled himself, there was some windfall to being the phantom, uncounted tenth man. Services would have to wait the few minutes it would take the reservist to arrive. Moving briskly to the bookshelf, Ovadyah resumed his review of the Torah portion.

It wasn't long before the perhaps less motivated but undeniably more Jewish tenth man arrived and services began. Ovadyah had become much more proficient in Hebrew over the past few months and was saying several of the prayers entirely in the original, even though Jewish law allowed for any language to be used. As he recited the portion of the *amidah*, or silent prayer, pertaining to material security, he paused to add a personal prayer in English. *That* was the Jewish response.

When services were over, Ovadyah wished everyone a good morning and instinctively rushed out to his car, slowing down only when, several feet from his vehicle, he suddenly remembered that he hadn't a reason in the world to rush. For the first time in years, he was a man with time to spare. Maybe it's God's way of providing me some extra time to study Torah and prepare for conversion, he told himself with a smile that quickly faded as he stopped to consider the true profundity of the notion.

Breakfast was on the table when he arrived home and the twins were readying themselves for school. Watching Ariella hurriedly finishing her coffee in preparation for her own dash off to work only deepened Ovadyah's gloom.

A half-hour later, the kids had gone off to school and Ariella to work. Ovadyah sat scribbling numbers on a small pad of paper. His countenance was a grim counterpoint to the smiley face printed at the top of the page. No way on earth, he told himself resignedly, can we keep the house under the circumstances and still eat. He picked up the phone and called an acquaintance who worked in real estate.

His soul itched to study, to use every moment his joblessness afforded him to prepare for his conversion, but his sense of responsibility to his family kept knocking at his mind's door like a pale, persistent missionary. Moving quickly and with determination, he went to the den, sat down at his typewriter and updated his resumé. Then he put his coat on, ran out to buy a paper, returned and opened it to the want ads. Within two hours, four manila envelopes lay on the kitchen table, sealed, addressed and stamped, and Ovadyah was at his desk in the den with a *chumash*, a Bible.

CHAPTER 22

Impending Events

Why put yourself through it all?" the white-smocked man across the desk said with an intense mixture of concern and exasperation. "You've got a beautiful family already!"

"Doctor," Ariella replied quietly but firmly, "I don't think I could really explain it to you." She thought a moment and then added, "Nor do I think I need to."

Thrusting his wizened hands into the pockets of his smock, Doctor Thurston Madison sank into a rare, wounded silence.

Ariella sometimes wondered why she stuck with the old fellow. He was getting on in years and seemed to be growing more crotchety with the passage of time. Still, she was used to him, and his occasional stubbornness and sermonizing didn't detract from his well-deserved reputation as a capable and experienced gynecologist-obstetrician. She really couldn't see herself starting anew with somebody else.

"Look," the doctor tried again, recouping his strength, "you've already been through the first battery of tests. You know they're no fun."

Tell me about it, Ariella thought, wincing imperceptibly at the memory of the procedures she had endured over the months since she'd first approached the doctor about reversing her sterilization. "And the signs so far," he continued, "are simply not very encouraging. Tubal ligation is a permanent decision, and it's one you made years ago. Everything we've seen to date indicates that you're not the best candidate for microsurgical repair."

"But you admit it's not an entirely futile hope."

"Of course it's not," he said resignedly, "but it just doesn't make any sense for you."

"That's *my* decision, Doctor," Ariella said, trying to smile through her tightly pursed lips.

The doctor dropped his voice an octave in an attempt to sound authoritative and reassuring at the same time.

"Ariella," he said slowly and deliberately, "you have to realize that I have a responsibility not only to you and your wishes, but to my own profession and ideals as well. I cannot and will not encourage or perform unnecessary surgery."

He paused a moment, seeming to search for the right phrase, and then, all pretense to reassurance vanishing, the words "*Pointless* surgery!" exploded from his lips.

An uneasy silence ensued before Ariella spoke again.

"Are you saying you won't continue the evaluation?"

The doctor sat stony-faced and quiet for a moment and Ariella thought she sensed some hesitation, some break in the clouds of his obstinacy. But she was wrong.

"Ariella," he continued softly, "I have always valued you as a patient. It's just that I can't justify this bizarre quest of yours for more children, not logically, medically or morally."

"Thank you all the same," Ariella said with a sigh as she rose to leave, "for your time, effort and concern."

Then, as she reached the door, she turned and addressed the doctor again.

"You may know your medicine," she said, almost in a whisper, "but logic and morality are, I'm afraid, not part of your expertise."

Ariella left the room and then the building, heading for the parking lot. Minutes later, safely enveloped in the soft space of her car, nurtured by its familiar smell and feel, she felt her stoicism melt into salty tears.

Even as her feelings bled from her eyes, though, her mind was consoling her. Obstacles, some part of her recalled, were intrinsic to human growth. Sometimes they were surmountable, sometimes not, but their existence and challenge were what the big game was all about. That idea, Ariella knew, underlay all of Jewish thought and life. She remembered once discussing with Ovadyah how poignant it was that the Jewish forefather Abraham, whose very essence was kindness and concern for others, had been commanded to evict his wife Hagar and his son Ishmael, and then to kill his son Isaac. What more outrageous trials of will could there possibly have been for a man like him?

And *she* thought *she* had problems? Was *she* being asked to sacrifice a child? In a way, yes, Ariella thought with a wry, unhappy smile. In a way, if she accepted Madison's prognosis as the final word. But she wasn't quite at that point yet. She still had to give things her best shot, to keep on pushing.

After several minutes, Ariella felt better. The cry seemed to have vented her smothering sorrow and allowed her soul to breathe again. Anyway, she told herself, she *had* to feel better. Ovadyah was still jobless and the family was about to move to a much smaller abode in a depressed and depressing neighborhood. Only her husband's impending conversion and whatever cheer she herself managed to muster kept a dark cloud of gloom at bay. She thought the words again: she *had* to feel better.

Returning home, Ariella found Ovadyah on the phone with Rabbi Solomon, talking about their upcoming trip to New York for the conversion. The date was only a week away and Ovadyah's excitement had become almost palpable.

Ariella tried to absorb some of it herself, to find the right wavelength and resonate with her husband's vibrancy. But as soon as he hung up and looked at her, he could tell she was hurting. "What's wrong?" he asked point-blank.

"I quit Dr. Madison," she said coolly, glad the tears had come and gone in the car. "The old goat and I have discovered — oh, how shall I put it? — some deep philosophical differences."

"I take it he didn't want to go ahead with things?"

Ariella nodded her confirmation.

"So where do we go from here?" he asked quietly.

"I wish I knew," she replied, quieter still.

They both knew there were plenty of doctors around but neither had a clue whom to approach — or if anyone else would be different from Madison.

"Ariella, I don't mean to harp on it but you know there's no need for you to try to change things. Nothing in Judaism — Rabbi Solomon assured us — and nothing in me — *I* assure you — is in any way pressuring you here."

The thought of another child did excite Ovadyah, but he squelched the electricity whenever he felt it buzz. It was hard enough consoling Ariella about her condition, especially since it was self-induced. He didn't need to fan his own spark into a flame, to wrestle with the angel of his own inner stirring. And he would certainly not badger his wife into anything.

"I know," Ariella said emphatically, "but something in *me* is pressuring me. And hard."

Ariella's desire for another child had blossomed over the months, doubling and quadrupling like the magically galvanized single cell it incessantly evoked in her imagination. The idea of children as the future had always been an intellectual truism for her, but the reality of the fact, its utter and undeniable *tangibility*, had been haunting her more and more intensely each day. How ironic, she reflected, how feminism had robbed her of her femininity, how it had made her subvert her most powerful possession as a woman. Her old N.O.W. cronies, she now realized, were never true feminists. A true feminist knows the power of a child, the power of a family. *She*

143

was a true feminist, and a victim of impostors.

Ariella had repeatedly told herself how futile her hope to bear another child was, how unimportant her desire, how it misled her, prevented her from focusing on the business of life. But like miniature tanks, the ubiquitous Boro Park baby carriages had overrun her heart's last outposts of denial. For her, another child *was* the business of life.

After several long moments, Ovadyah's voice finally penetrated her depression.

"Ar?"

"Hmm?"

"I have an idea. *If*, that is, you're still determined to keep at it."

She looked at him, hopeful and skeptical put together.

"The last time I was at Rabbi Solomon's house studying with him," her husband recollected, "he got a phone call from some rabbi in Boston who is apparently well-known for his medical connections. It seems that he helps people with special medical needs."

Ariella was intrigued.

"Maybe," Ovadyah went on, "he could refer us to someone top-notch with the right attitude. At the very least, if a doctor he recommended also maintained that it was pointless, we'd know for sure, once and for all."

Ariella didn't say anything but her eyes told her husband to get right to work, and he did.

Rabbi Solomon was well aware of Ariella's plight, and when he took Ovadyah's call, his eyebrows shot up at the request that came through the receiver.

"That's wild, Ovadyah," he said. "Honestly, I was thinking of getting in touch with the Bostoner for you even before you called."

"With the who?" Ovadyah asked.

"I'm sorry," he chuckled. "'The Bostoner' is the Bostoner Rebbe. He's a really wonderful person — he cares deeply for every Jew and has helped countless people through difficult times."

"Does he do miracles?" Ovadyah asked drolly, knowing that Chassidic rebbes were often reputed to have supernatural abilities. "Because we sure could use one."

"Listen," the rabbi said, "just about a week from now, you'll be performing one of your own. You'll be creating a new Jew. May one miracle lead to another."

"Amen," Ovadyah seconded the rabbi's blessing. "So how do we get in touch with the Rebbe?"
"Well, let me make the first call and see if I can't get things moving for you," Rabbi Solomon

said. "The Rebbe's usually very busy and he shuttles between Israel and the States. I'll get back to you as soon as I get through to him."

A half-hour later, Rabbi Solomon was explaining Ovadyah and Ariella's situation to the Rebbe. Having met the Bostoner on several occasions, Rabbi Solomon had found him entirely unpretentious and utterly sincere. Never aloof, he always had a broad, warm smile for everyone. His white beard was not that of an angry prophet but that of a loving grandfather. And constantly underscoring his simple friendliness was his anomalous lack of any European accent. Though he looked like an "old world" Chassidic rebbe, he was wholly American, born and bred. That was partly how he had attracted so many Jewish college students to his Chassidic stream and how he had become so widely respected among New England's Jewish intelligentsia.

While he was always willing to counsel anyone who needed his spiritual services, the Rebbe never insinuated himself more than necessary into situations where medical attention was the immediate need. In such cases, he was gratified to play the "matchmaker," introducing patient to doctor. Drawing on his extensive connections in the New England medical community, the Bostoner often referred Jews in need of medical care to those who could best provide it.

Rabbi Solomon expected true empathy and concrete help from the Rebbe, and he got both. The conversation wasn't long but it was full. Soon, he called Ovadyah back with the name of a fertility specialist. "But no guarantees," he cautioned.

There were no guarantees — but at last there was a glimmer of hope.

CHAPTER 23

Aqueous Solution

The trip seemed interminable. Ovadyah was overjoyed that the day had arrived, that he was finally taking his last ride as a non-Jew. But his sights were really set on the day *after* his conversion, when it would all be behind him.

The previous week had been a long and busy one, with the painful move to the apartment and a hasty trip to Boston to meet with the specialist the Bostoner Rebbe had suggested.

The doctor had impressed the Gomeses as helpful, positive and expert, just as they'd hoped, though it had come as a disconcerting surprise that he intended to repeat all the tests and procedures Ariella had already been subjected to. He wanted, he said, to make sure everything was in order before performing any expensive, involved surgery. It would be silly, he told them, to proceed if all their efforts were likely doomed from the start.

Ariella, though, Ovadyah recalled with a silent chuckle, had set the fellow straight. None too gently, she'd reminded him that all the tests he was planning had already been run, and that most of the results had been, if not perfect, at least satisfactory. She'd told him further that she wouldn't be growing any younger waiting for all the retests and their results.

A bit taken aback, yet oddly pleased at her insistence, the doctor had agreed to accept Dr. Madison's results. Fifteen minutes later, he had secured a date for the operation. The big day, he'd said, "with the Lord's help," would be in five weeks.

Now, as Rabbi Solomon's van carried him down the highway, Ovadyah marveled at Ariella's determination. When she believed in something, or wanted something badly enough, there was no standing in her way. He really admired that. She had decided not to come along on the "conversion trip," as they'd called it, and he missed her already.

The white lines on the road, approaching warily and then darting beneath them, had a stuporous effect on Ovadyah. He had hardly slept the past few nights and now dozed off in mid-thought. He slept for a long time, and the next thing he heard was Rabbi Solomon's cheerful announcement that "We're here!"

"Here" was a nondescript building in Brooklyn that housed a *mikvah*, or ritual bath. Ovadyah blinked several times and shook his head to make sure he was fully awake as the rabbi parked the car. A moment later, the two men entered the building.

"Rabbi Schechter has arranged everything for us," Rabbi Solomon explained to his charge, "use of the facilities, the *mohel*, the witnesses. So your conversion will have his reputation behind it." That was reassuring, Ovadyah thought. He didn't need another quasi-conversion. This was to be it, the real thing. Not only would he himself know he was a genuine Jew, every other Jew — even the most pious and demanding — would know it, too.

Several minutes later, a young man of nineteen or twenty, sporting a scraggly beard and a nervous smile, introduced himself as one of the witnesses for the conversion procedure.

Any official change of status within Judaism, Ovadyah knew well, required the presence of two adult, male witnesses. The inclusion of a third man would create a *beis din*, a court, to preside over the conversion.

The fellow was pleasant and articulate as he related how he was a student in Rabbi Schechter's yeshivah, how he was very close to him, and how Rabbi Schechter had asked him and a friend to participate in the conversion. The young man told Ovadyah and Rabbi Solomon that he had been greatly honored by the offer, that he had felt it was a wonderful opportunity to be part of something truly important. Earnestness beamed from his eyes as he spoke and Ovadyah felt honored himself.

He followed the fellow upstairs and into a room. Two men stood within, a young man Ovadyah took to be his escort's friend — the second witness — and a shirtsleeved, bent-over, elderly man with a long, gray beard and antiquated pince-nez — a caretaker or maybe a retired scholar, he imagined. Ovadyah wondered where the *mohel* was.

He didn't wonder long. The fellow who had fetched him from the lobby gently guided him to where the old man stood and introduced him as Rabbi Pinsker, "who will be performing the hatafah."

Well, Ovadyah thought, I certainly hope he isn't as unskilled as he looks. Why, he's positively *ancient*! Can he *see*? Can he actually wield a *scalpel*?

Ovadyah tried not to let his thoughts influence his face as he said, "Pleased to meet you," and extended the *mohel* his hand.

Rabbi Pinsker nodded a wordless hello and offered Ovadyah a limp handshake. The man's long moustache may have harbored a small smile but Ovadyah wasn't sure. Nor was he very reassured — and he groped for some way to ascertain that he could be at ease with the ritual circumcisor into whose hands he had been entrusted.

147

"Uh, are you...very experienced?" he asked haltingly.

When no response was forthcoming, he fumbled for other words.

"I mean, have you done this many times before?"

The *mohel* glared at him, the silence deafening.

"Please to excuse me," he said, addressing Ovadyah with more than a trace of a European accent and none whatsoever of a smile. "I have been *mohel* for over fifty years. EXPERT *mohel*."

And thus began a long lecture about Rabbi Pinsker's training at the hands of some famous rabbi Ovadyah had never heard of and the unparalleled importance of years of experience in the field of ritual circumcision. Ovadyah was sincerely sorry he had thought to question his host.

He was directed to a table of the sort found in doctors' examining rooms, a tall, padded affair complete with the requisite sheet of white paper along its length. Rabbi Pinsker motioned to him to climb up, which he did. Removing his clothing from the waist down, Ovadyah tried to focus on the fact that he'd be properly converted and out of the place in a half-hour.

Lying supine on the table, a clean sheet covering him, and watching the *mohel* carefully wash his hands, Ovadyah had to admit that the fellow seemed professional. He had carefully laid out various bottles and instruments — things he would not likely need for so simple a procedure — and the energy with which the old man scrubbed and moved belied his apparent antiquity. Ovadyah laid back and waited.

Finally, the sound of water stopped and the mohel was standing next to him.

"You know Shema?" he asked, referring not only to the basic Jewish credo, "Hear O Israel, the Lord is our God, the Lord is One," but to the lengthy compendium of verses observant Jews read along with it twice daily.

Ovadyah felt like delivering a lecture of his own to his suddenly tall inquisitor, informing him that his patient had been observant for months and had known the entire Shema by heart even longer. All he said, though, was "Yes."

"Good," Rabbi Pinsker replied, sounding a bit more human. "Is good for you to say Shema while I am doing the *hatafah*."

Rabbi Pinsker lifted the sheet and the two witnesses moved closer. Even flat on his back, Ovadyah could clearly see their faces, and he felt very uncomfortable at their concentration on him. Goodness, he thought, they were more than just a presence in the room. They were...they were *witnessing*. He wanted to fidget at the thought, but did not dare.

Ovadyah's discomfort, however, was nothing compared to what followed. After a momentary, cold touch — which was annoying enough — he suddenly felt a sharp pain. That was no pinch, his mind gasped, no cakewalk like in Rabbi Shoman's office at Beth Am. This guy had really *cut* him, for heaven's sake!

148

Then, just as he was collecting the words to ask what in tarnation was going on and could it please stop immediately, he felt something cool and soothing where the echoes of pain had just been. Bravely lifting his head, he saw the mohel salving and bandaging the incision he had made. The two witnesses looked pale. He also saw a blood-stained scalpel lying on a white sheet draping a small table.

"Everything is fine," Rabbi Pinsker informed his charge.

Easy for you to say, buddy, Ovadyah thought, but at the same time he felt indebted to the *mohel* for a *hatafah* that he *knew* had met the most exacting standards.

"Please to lie here a few minutes," the mohel continued. "Bandage is just to stop the bleeding. We take it off before you go into *mikvah*."

Ovadyah knew that immersion in a *mikvah* was effective only if one's body was completely free of dirt or other intervening substances. He wondered if the cut could really handle the water so soon, but the pain had definitely subsided. Maybe, he thought, he hadn't been so grievously wounded after all, and the mere shock of being cut was what had so discomfitted him.

As Ovadyah reminded himself that the worst was over and the moment of conversion was imminent, his spirits lifted. He lay there with the sheet pulled up to his waist for what seemed a long time but he felt no impatience, only calm.

When the mohel removed the bandage, Ovadyah instinctively greeted him with a smile. To his surprise, it was immediately returned.

Ovadyah sat up gingerly and realized with some amazement that he was not incapacitated. He dressed and followed the *mohel* and witnesses out of the room. He was then shown to a dressing room and shower adjoining the *mikvah*.

He undressed, this time completely, and after showering and checking every inch of his body for any foreign, intervening substances, he opened the door to the mikvah. A steamy warmth hit him squarely and before him, sunken into the floor, lay the deep, square-tiled ritual bath. Lights recessed into the ceiling played on the surface of the clear, warm water, and though he was alone in the room, Ovadyah felt suddenly exposed and vulnerable. He wanted desperately to descend the steps that led into the water and let the mikvah engulf him, clothing him with its shimmering, ethereal reflections.

Another door suddenly opened and Ovadyah jumped. Just the inquisition, he joked wryly to himself, meaning the two witnesses and the *mohel*.

"Ah, you beat us!" the *mohel* said with a more jovial face than Ovadyah would have wagered the man possessed. "We went to your rabbi to let him know where we holding."

While he spoke, the *mohel* looked down into the water of the *mikvah*, as did the others, averting their gaze from the man who had brought them together that day. Now, though, as the moment of immersion grew near, they turned to face their subject.

"Please to go in," Rabbi Pinsker said quietly, almost solemnly, "till the neck."

Ovadyah quickly descended the steps. He imagined six eyes following him every inch of the way. Finally, the warm water enveloped him like a mother's hug. When it reached his neck, he turned to face what had now become three pairs of shoes in his line of sight.

"Mr. Gomes," came one of the witnesses' voices, "do you realize what you are undertaking by becoming a Jew?"

Before Ovadyah could respond, the young man continued.

"You will be obligated to keep all the Torah's laws, from those like tzitzis and tefillin — "
Ovadyah had been wearing the fringed garment and phylacteries for months now.

" — to the complicated and important laws of Shabbos and holidays."

Complicated was right, Ovadyah thought. Back in their Beth Am days, he and Ariella had thought that turning the oven on before sunset granted carte blanche for any cooking on the Sabbath day. Boy, had they been ignorant, he sighed to himself.

"You don't have to know everything at once, of course," the voice went on, "but you have to accept everything at once now — both the things you already know and the things you'll learn as you go on."

After a pause, the feet continued.

"And you must realize, too, that the Jewish lot is not always a pleasant one. Jews are hated by many, sometimes persecuted, even attacked."

Ovadyah thought back to what he had learned in college about the Jews in Spain and Portugal, where his own roots ran.

"Do you still want to go ahead with the *tevilah* and *geirus*?" The voice posed the question slowly and clearly.

"Yes," Ovadyah replied without hesitation.

Then the voice said something that sent a shiver through him even in the warm, comforting water. Though the words carried no real surprise, they shocked him as if the tiny sea in which he stood had suddenly become electrified.

"Mr. Gomes," the voice intoned, each syllable a jolt, "this is it; *after this, there is no turning back.*"

No turning back. The words reverberated within Ovadyah's mind, their implications screaming from what seemed every direction. He mentally repeated the phrase. A momentary dunking of his head and he would be Jewish, Jewish without question and beyond doubt. He would never be able to return to his non-Jewish state. If he were to abandon Judaism in the future, he would become not a gentile again but an apostate Jew. In the past, that thought had always been reassuring. Yet as he stood there in the ritual bath, a mere bend of the knees between him and a lifelong identity as a Jew, it had become somehow overwhelming, striking, frightening.

"I understand," he said, hoping his fear didn't show.

"When you go beneath the water," the voice concluded, "close your mouth and eyes but not tightly, and lift your feet off the floor for a moment."

Ovadyah took a deep breath, followed his orders, submerged his head and became a Jew.

CHAPTER 24

Mazel Tov!

Emerging from the *mikvah*, eyes still closed and water dripping from his face, Ovadyah heard an ill-tuned chorus of hearty "mazel tovs." Blinking away the drops and craning his head, he glimpsed the three smiling faces of his "Jewish court."

"We'll wait for you in the main lobby," one of the witnesses said.

And with that they exited the room, leaving Ovadyah alone with the sound of the sloshing mini-surf he had created upon surfacing. Before leaving the mikvah, he went under one more time but failed to recapture the visceral rush of his first immersion.

Ascending the steps into a new and chilly world, Ovadyah glanced back at the water and imagined part of himself left behind, trapped forever beneath the surface, buried at sea. The *mikvah*, he knew, would remain unaffected by the dunking, like some spiritual black hole, but his past had indeed been irretrievably shed into the shimmering pool.

Ovadyah quickly toweled, dressed and returned to the lobby, where Rabbi Solomon fell on him with a long, hard bear hug. "Mazel tov, Ovadyah!" he said over and over.

When Rabbi Solomon finally released him, Ovadyah turned to the two witnesses, who seemed amused at the attack as they sang a song whose most prominent phrase was "Mazel tov!" The *mohel* was sitting at a desk, scrutinizing and occasionally scribbling on a preprinted Hebrew form.

"I want to thank you all very much," Ovadyah addressed the threesome.

"Thank *you*, Mr. Gomes," the young man who had first fetched him demurred, his friend nodding in agreement. "It was an honor to be part of your *geirus*."

The friend, who hadn't spoken the entire time, grabbed Ovadyah's hand, shook it warmly and added, "Welcome to Klal Yisrael!"

Rabbi Pinsker, still seated at the desk with pen in hand, peered over his archaic eyeglasses at Ovadyah.

"Now," he exclaimed, a wide smile intruding on his stern demeanor, "is everything official!" Rising energetically from his seat, he brandished the form he had been filling out and handed it to Ovadyah.

Ovadyah took the document, shook the *mohel's* hand and returned his smile. Rabbi Solomon thanked Rabbi Pinsker as well, and then the two visitors bid their hosts goodbye.

Outside, the air smelled so fresh that Ovadyah had to force himself into Rabbi Solomon's van. With the slam of his door, Rabbi Solomon turned to him and asked, "Nu, now that you've 'arrived,' what's the first thing you want to do as a Jew?"

Ovadyah thought about it only a moment before the obvious dawned.

"Learn," he answered simply.

Rabbi Solomon beamed and headed off for Yeshivas Chaim Berlin, the rabbinical college headed by Rabbi Schechter. He hoped that the rabbi would be available to speak with them for a few minutes, just to congratulate Ovadyah on his conversion — that would really be a precious welcome into the Jewish world.

When they arrived at the yeshivah and entered the crowded study hall, or *beis medrash*, Ovadyah was visibly struck. It was like walking onto the floor of a skullcapped New York Stock Exchange. Though most of the hundreds of young men in the large room were sitting or standing in place, there was commotion everywhere: hands flew through the air, bodies rocked back and forth intently, and heads shook "yes," "no" and other, stranger responses.

The backdrop for all the frenzied movement was a din the likes of which Ovadyah had never heard before. At first, it seemed a silly buzz of the cocktail party variety, but then various singsongs began to emerge from the chaos, randomly mingling with one another. It was something like a large, frenetic orchestra tuning up without end.

Even more striking, no one seemed to notice their entry into the large room; the mass of movement and sound paid as much attention to their presence as the ocean would to a pair of pier holes in the surf.

Ovadyah was anxious to take advantage of their happy oblivion and melt into the cacophonous study wave that washed across the room. "Let's sit down and learn," he half-suggested, half-ordered Rabbi Solomon, who immediately went to a nearby bookshelf and procured two volumes. They were Mishnayos, containing the earliest Talmudic material, the laws constituting the nucleus of the Oral Law. The two men found seats at the end of a crowded table, opened their books and, with Rabbi Solomon leading, began to carefully study the arcane text.

No sooner had they started to make some headway in delineating the limitations on a sukkah's height than they sensed something black and fluid wavering nearby. Though they both tried to concentrate on the Hebrew words in front of them, a sudden, local hole in the wall of sound made them look up. Ovadyah immediately recognized Rabbi Schechter's radiant face, long, albescent beard and beaming, warm smile. Following Rabbi Solomon's lead, he quickly rose to his feet in the presence of the respected sage.

"Shalom aleichem!" the *rosh yeshivah* greeted them, each syllable seeming to reach out and embrace them.

The two visitors each shook the older man's outstretched hand.

"I was hoping you'd come here after the *geirus*," the elder rabbi said with a twinkle in his eye. Then he turned to Ovadyah and boomed with almost palpable joy, "Mazel tov! So how did things go?"

Suddenly uncomfortable with the realization that dozens of eyes had fixed on him, the new ger answered a quiet "Baruch Hashem."

"Could we talk for a few minutes?" the *rosh yeshivah* inquired.

The invitation seemed directed to Ovadyah alone, but Rabbi Solomon's happiness for him squelched any disappointment he might have felt at being left out.

"With your permission, of course," Rabbi Schechter added, nodding toward Rabbi Solomon.

"Certainly!" he responded with a slightly embarrassed smile.

The *rosh yeshivah* took Ovadyah by the arm and led him into a nondescript office. Motioning his guest to an upholstered chair, the older man took his own seat behind a spartan desk on which a dozen or so Hebrew volumes lay scattered. "This," he said, displaying one of them, "is a *Rambam*. Do you know who the Rambam was?"

Rambam, Ovadyah silently recalled: Rabbi Moshe ben Maimon; born in Spain, died in Egypt in 1204; arguably the most famous of the medieval scholars of Jewish law; magnum opus: Mishneh Torah, often simply called "the Rambam."

"Yes," Ovadyah answered.

"I would like to learn some important excerpts from the Rambam with you today since I don't know when I'll see you next. I also want to give you some advice and the opportunity to ask me any questions you might have. Being Jewish, you must remember, means always asking questions. Without questions, there can be no growth, and to be a Jew is to constantly seek to grow."

With that, Rabbi Schechter opened the book he had taken in hand and read from it aloud, carefully translating each Hebrew phrase. He read first about a convert's status as a "newborn child" whose past has effectively ceased to exist, then about how conversion to Judaism is irreversible — Ovadyah thought back to how the finality of his Jewishness had hit him as he'd stood in the *mikvah* — and finally about how a convert shares the exact same benefits and responsibilities as any Jew. Rabbi Schechter noted how often converts are mentioned in the Torah in connection to so many varied laws, their status as full Jews thereby emphasized beyond all doubt. He explained further how, in Biblical times, a semi-convert status was available to non-Jews who accepted a relationship with the Jewish people but did not actually become part of it.

"You, though, Ovadyah," he went on, "have joined us entirely; with your unconditional acceptance of mitzvos, you have fully and truly become a Jew."

He told Ovadyah that there were two distinct commandments in the Torah to love a convert: the basic commandment to love every Jew, and a special mitzvah to love a *ger*.

Then came the advice. The *rosh yeshivah*'s voice grew quiet, yet in Ovadyah's mind, it thundered.

"Ovadyah, there's a world of opportunity out there, but for a Jew, there's a world of *shmutz*, too." Ovadyah puzzled at the funny word.

"Shmutz literally means `dirt,'" Rabbi Schechter explained, "but what I mean by a world of *shmutz* is the constant barrage of profane attitudes and images people live with these days.

"Our society has no real morality. What it calls freedom is only anarchy, and lewdness is its idea of beauty. As a Jew, Ovadyah, you have a vital responsibility to recognize the Jewish people's greatest enemy, a threat more dangerous than any sort of anti-Semitism could possibly be. The adversary is the spiritual corruption of the society we live in. You must resist it at every turn. If you're not constantly on guard to keep it out of your home and your heart, it will undoubtedly seep in unnoticed. That's its great strength: its stealth. No one can really escape its onslaught, but if you recognize its attack, and if you're careful, you can keep it at bay."

Ovadyah had always understood that being a Jew entailed something of a separation from society at large. After all, a truly Jewish life had little in common with Western ideals and aspirations. But he had never really felt the *threat* of the non-Jewish milieu quite as Rabbi Schechter had described it. He knew, though, that the advice was good and savored the elder's words, absorbing the simple but vital truths they carried.

The rabbi spoke about other challenging areas of Jewish life, about the detailed and important Sabbath laws, and about the vital need to educate Jewish children at home as well as in school. Then he asked Ovadyah if he had any concerns or questions of his own.

He did have a question, as it happened.

Ovadyah knew well that there were distinct, sometimes striking variations in the style, wording and pronunciation of the liturgy among Jews with roots in different parts of the world. Eastern European Jews of non-Chassidic persuasion read and do things one way; Chassidic Jews another. Sephardic Jews, whose ancestors came from the Iberian peninsula, have a different nusach, or text of prayer, from their Ashkenazic counterparts. Italian Jews have yet another, Yemenite Jews still another. Since prayer is so central to Jewish life, Ovadyah was concerned about which *nusach* and pronunciation he should use. Since his own roots stretched to Portugal, should he adopt the Sephardic approach to Jewish liturgy and custom?

After a pensive pause, Rabbi Schechter asked his guest where he <%0>would most often be davening in Hope Heights.

"At the Hope Heights Hebrew Day School minyan," he replied. That was where Rabbi Solomon and many of his friends davened, and where Ovadyah felt most comfortable.

"And what custom is used there?"

"Ashkenaz."

"Then you should take on the Ashkenazic custom," the rabbi said<%0> quietly but resolutely. "Your roots are of no halachic consequence and it is imperative that you be perceived — and perceive *yourself* — as a full member of your Jewish community. The last thing you need is to set yourself apart in any way from your fellow Jews."

Ovadyah liked the sound of the rabbi's last phrase.

After Rabbi Schechter spent a few more minutes explaining how essentially minor the differences in custom were, he jumped a bit as he glanced at the clock on the wall.

"Ovadyah," he said, "forgive me, I have an important appointment now. But I want you to know that I'm always available to you should any questions arise."

"Thank you, Rebbe," Ovadyah answered wholeheartedly. "I appreciate that very much — and thank you for your time."

The two men rose and Rabbi Schechter shook Ovadyah's hand warmly, continuing to hold it even as they emerged from the office. The sight of the almost luminously white-bearded older man and the dark-haired, dark-skinned younger one hand in hand as they reentered the study hall might have struck some as odd, but neither man felt in the least self-conscious.

Ovadyah scanned the large hall, finally spying Rabbi Solomon's yarmulke. The skullcap was all that was visible of his mentor, for his forehead was resting on his folded arms, which in turn rested on the open pages of the book he had been studying.

The two newcomers to the room walked over to the obviously exhausted man beneath the yarmulke and Rabbi Schechter tapped him on the shoulder. Rabbi Solomon lifted his head. Though at first he saw only one swarthy blur and one light one, he quickly surmised what they were and rose to his feet.

"Oy!" he said, trying to get his eyes to focus. "I think the trip must have caught up with me!"

"Mitzvos can be draining experiences," the rosh yeshivah assured him with a smile. "There is actually no better way to be overcome by needed sleep than by trying to fight it off by learning. Both of you should rest before your trip home. Are you staying the night?"

"No, Rebbe," Rabbi Solomon replied. "I've got to be at school tomorrow. But we'll be refreshed after we have dinner."

"I hope so," Rabbi Schechter said, "though I'd feel much better if you stayed overnight. In any event, please drive carefully. And slowly."

Rabbi Solomon blushed at the admonition, having driven Rabbi Schechter around Hope Heights when the *rosh yeshivah* had visited.

"Thank you for everything," Rabbi Solomon said, shaking Rabbi Schechter's hand goodbye.

"Be well," the *rosh yeshivah* said in Yiddish. Then, with a final, blazing smile, he sat down and studied a text for several moments before leaving the room.

Rabbi Solomon explained to Ovadyah that, as a *beis medrash* possessed a special holiness, it was improper to enter it for mundane purposes alone. If one came in, for instance, to see or talk to someone, he should at least learn something before leaving. That was what Rabbi Schechter was doing.

Ovadyah found nothing odd about the explanation; he had sensed the holiness of the place the moment he'd walked in.

"So," Rabbi Solomon exclaimed, having finally fully returned to the world of the woken, "what should we eat? Italian? Morrocan?"

Ovadyah was surprised to find himself suddenly hungry, and as his watch had been in his jacket pocket since the *mikvah*, he asked Rabbi Solomon what time it was.

"Just after seven," came the reply.

"How long was I in there with Rabbi Schechter?" he inquired, puzzled.

"Just over two hours," he answered.

Ovadyah was flabbergasted. He would have guessed twenty minutes, at most a half-hour.

"Nu, what'll it be?" Rabbi Solomon persisted.

"Huh?"

"For our celebration, what'll it be? Morrocan? French? French-Morrocan maybe?"

Ovadyah chuckled as he finally found his host's wavelength. Jokingly, he said, "Chinese."

"Great!" came the immediate and enthusiastic reply. "I know a fantastic place called `Yid Fress

Chow' that's not five minutes from here!"

Could be worse, I suppose, thought Ovadyah, suppressing a hearty laugh.

CHAPTER 25

Home Stretch

It was hard to believe the wait was nearly over; all three months of separation had elapsed but for one week — Ovadyah had now been a Jew for two. He didn't *look* any different, Ariella mused; he didn't even *act* differently since his conversion. But then, he'd already been observant for months

Though she tried not to, Ariella surveyed the apartment again. The move had gone as smoothly as one could expect but the place was horribly small and even more horribly drab. It was affordable, though, on the single income that was sustaining them, and that was all that mattered for the moment.

The kitchen, where she sat, was particularly depressing. The strips of paint peeling from its walls seemed to mock her like so many protruding tongues.

Just then, Ovadyah returned from afternoon services, pulled off his tie as if it were a noose, and sat down opposite his wife.

"O brave, strong hunter of employment," she addressed the intrusion on her thoughts, "captured any prey today?"

"Not even anybody's attention," Ovadyah replied without much disappointment. At times, Ariella felt he had acclimated to rejection. "Not to fear, though, great nurturer and provider for us all!" he continued, rising from his seat. "I have some promising leads for future hunts."

Ariella felt some relief at his optimism, though she wondered how realistic it was. Still, in the depths of her heart, she, too, was confident that things would turn out okay, that they had no right to feel abandoned or hopeless just because Ovadyah was out of work. God, she had slowly but surely learned, had His own plans for men and women, and while they sometimes suspected Him of sleeping on the job, He never was.

159

"I saw Rabbi Solomon at services," Ovadyah went on as he moved to the counter and put up some coffee. "He told me that the evening after the last day of our three months, we should come to the school so he can perform a wedding ceremony."

"To make us official, huh?"

"Hey, it's high time you married a Jewish guy, don't you think?"

Ariella laughed and reflected on the fact that she was about to marry the same man for the third time. Back at the beginning, there had been the justice of the peace. Then, when they had joined Beth Am, there had been a brief renewal of vows in Rabbi Shoman's office — and now this re-renewal.

Ariella remembered the Beth Am ceremony well; it had taken place during their lunch break. In attendance were Rabbi Shoman, Rabbi Allen and the twins, the latter summoned at the last minute from the Finkelstein School for the occasion. Rabbi Shoman chanted some blessings over a cup of wine, Ovadyah broke the traditional glass with his foot, the twins were sent back to school and the newlyweds went home for lunch.

"Who's going to be there?" Ariella asked. "Just Rabbi Solomon?"

"Well, he'll be performing the wedding and there'll have to be two witnesses, of course. And he asked if we wanted to invite a few more people — you know, Ron and Dina, a couple of the rabbis from Hope Heights Hebrew and their wives — just to make it a little more than a bare-bones ceremony."

"I suppose our folks should be there, too," Ariella pointed out. "And the twins, of course."

"Of course."

"That's Monday night, right?"

"Don't be late."

"You, either," Ariella said through a smile.

"Well," she said after a moment, "we'd better get ready or we'll be late for our dinner engagement."

Ovadyah's raised eyebrows signaled his incomprehension.

"Remember, dear?" Ariella helped him along. "The Rosens? It's Monday — we're invited for dinner."

"Oh yes, of course I remember!" Ovadyah exclaimed in an exaggerated, obvious lie.

As he reknotted his tie, Ariella searched for a hat to match her outfit. Though the idea of a *sheitel*, or wig, still seemed a bit radical for her taste, she had taken to wearing hats in deference to the halachah prohibiting the display of a married woman's hair in public.

Within minutes, Ariella's head was covered, Ovadyah's neck was renoosed, the kids were in the car and they were all on their way to the Rosens'. They made the trip in under ten minutes, an especially good sign, Ovadyah remarked.

"*Kefitzas haderech*," he explained, "'the shortening of the road' — a sign that God is guiding you."

Friendly and gracious as always, their hosts ushered them in and introduced them to another guest, a pleasant, middle-aged gentleman who seemed only vaguely knowledgeable about Judaism but greatly so about his hobby, real estate. Much of the conversation at the table was actually a monologue delivered by him about land, houses and interest rates. The Rosens let their guest talk on, though the topic clearly enthralled neither them nor the Gomeses.

During a lull in the lecture, just after Dina and Ron had brought the main course to the table, Ovadyah mentioned that he and Ariella had just sold their home and were now living in a rented place pending his hopeful reemployment.

The real estate agent looked up from his food.

"What'd you sell for?" he asked.

Ovadyah told him.

"What are you paying for rent?"

Ovadyah told him.

"Your present income?" the interrogator persisted.

Ovadyah hesitated a moment and then told him.

"Hey, listen, I know of a beautiful house right here on the West End that will be on the market within days. It's a two-family, but with a down payment like the one you guys could make plus rental income from the second apartment and the rent you're paying now, you could probably swing it."

Sure, thought Ovadyah.

"Really!" continued the inquisitor-turned-salesman as if he had read Ovadyah's mind. And then he went on to delineate all the pertinent facts and figures.

Ovadyah had to admit that it all sounded good. Very good, as a matter of fact, especially if he found employment soon. But he was far from sure just how much of the good was real and how much was wishful thinking. Glancing at Ariella, he was surprised to see that although her expression had previously registered only pained boredom and then — when the questions were

161

being fired — unmistakable umbrage, it had now metamorphosed into a cautious but clear look of piqued interest.

The Gomeses took the guy's number.

By Wednesday, one of Ovadyah's job leads showed some promise. A respected insurance firm was seeking to train financial planners, and he'd been called back for a second interview. Buoyed by the security that dangled before them like a lure, Ariella and Ovadyah decided to at least take a look at the place the Rosens' guest had mentioned.

It was indeed a lovely house, on a neat, quiet street. Furthermore, the neighborhood was precisely the one they wanted, well within walking distance of Hope Heights Hebrew, the Rosens' house and everything else they had come to value in recent months. But they both agreed that a commitment would be highly premature as long as Ovadyah's job was still in the nebulous realm of the merely possible. Besides, Ovadyah said, it somehow seemed like they should at least wait until their "three months" were up and they were a normal family again before making any big decisions.

It was, after all, only a matter of days.

CHAPTER 26

Holy Matrimony

"Spaceman" Mallory wondered what he was doing there; it wasn't exactly his usual sort of gig, to put it mildly. Spaceman — used to be Steve — had played most of the clubs in what passed for a downtown in Hope Heights, plus an occasional last-minute fill-in at a few Boston joints. But this gig was majorly weird, and it was all Frank's fault, bless his scraggly little beard.

Looking out over the crowd of what seemed like seventy or eighty people, the women in elegant, long-sleeved dresses, the men in suits, ties and black, felt hats — *hats*, for goodness sake! — Spaceman felt very, very out of place, even in the bow tie Frank had scrounged up for him.

He'd first met Frank in a music store about a year back. Spaceman had been playing around with a new Fender — his girlfriend had made off with his old piece and his wallet the day before — when suddenly this short, longish-haired Jewish guy — complete with beard and beanie — started eyeing him. Spaceman just ignored him at first but thought it was pretty cool when the little guy picked up a saxophone and started improvising in time and harmony with what he was playing. Spaceman got a little more elaborate, with some Pink Floyd and a couple of original riffs thrown in for good measure, but the dude just followed suit, grooving like a seasoned jazzman and jumping around like the floor was on fire. Spaceman was good but so was this guy, and the jam session went on, to the mild amusement of the other customers. Spaceman really freaked when the guy, still blowing at the sax like a hurricane, danced over to a display, took a violin and bow down and almost seamlessly switched instruments, staying with the guitar lead the whole way and impressively improvising whenever Spaceman gave him the opportunity. Next thing he knew, the guy with the beard was playing a piccolo — a *piccolo* — and they still sounded great together.

They got sort of friendly after that and Spaceman even got Frank hired once or twice to play with him. But Frank wouldn't perform in certain kinds of places — and wouldn't do Friday night jobs at all — so there weren't all that many opportunities for the guy. Spaceman liked him, though, and appreciated his straight, honest attitude toward life, even though the two really had nothing but music in common. Frank had explained that he was a religious Jew, but Spaceman didn't know much about religion. All he knew was that the guy was smart, talented and trustworthy. And that, Spaceman knew, made him a rare bird.

Which was why when Frank had asked Spaceman to help *him* with a gig — a *wedding*, of all things — the guitarist just couldn't refuse, even though the music for the night was pure freakiness, not one selection from his standard repertoire. Spaceman had to practice the melodic but not very sophisticated stuff for seven or eight sessions to get it down pat. Actually, every song revolved around only two or three chords, but he also had to remember exactly when each piece was to be played; the whole performance was sort of choreographed to be in sync with the ceremony. Luckily, he was a fast learner.

So here he was in some synagogue hall, wearing a bow tie and a beanie himself, waiting for the signal to play. The band consisted of the two of them and another Jewish guy — a *seminary student* was how Frank described him — a clean-cut, short-haired, '50s kind of dude who you'd never think would have the strength or coordination to drum like he did. Together, Spaceman marveled, they really didn't sound bad at all.

The men in the large room started filing out, and in minutes the musicians were the only males left. Some double doors at one side of the hall opened and the crowd of women began clapping in unison and escorting the bride in. Frank nodded and the trio began playing their first piece, following the tempo of the clapping. The bride, wearing a white dress and a lace veil, seemed surprised at the scene, which Spaceman thought odd — it *was* the lady's wedding, after all.

Frank nodded again, and just as the bride was seated on a chair in the middle of the room, the band launched into its second selection. The women rushed into a huddle, which quickly became a dance. Spaceman had been asked not to watch them as he played, lest it make them nervous, but he stole a few curious glances anyway, just to see what they were *doing*. First they formed a circle and then a second one inside the first, one moving clockwise, the other counterclockwise. They were keeping time with their steps and it was sort of nice, though hardly like the stuff Spaceman usually saw going down on a dance floor.

They played the same song over and over again. Unlike Spaceman, the women and girls on the floor didn't seem to tire of it.

Finally, Frank gave the signal for the next piece. It had a faster tempo and Spaceman was surprised at how lively, almost wild, the women got, even in their formal clothes. He felt a little unreal watching so many otherwise ladylike women of all ages whirling around like square dancers on speed.

Looking over at Frank, Spaceman saw that his friend had really gotten into the music himself. On the flute for this piece, Frank was swaying back and forth with his eyes shut tight. Though his lips were pinched tightly around the mouthpiece, he seemed to be smiling behind the instrument. The happiness was catching, Spaceman thought, and he felt himself moving and playing with a lot more feeling than the music justified.

164

Ovadyah and Ariella's first clue should have been all the cars parked in front of Hope Heights Hebrew. There must have been fifteen or twenty of them.

The second clue they missed was the explosion of happy noise that met them when they entered the building. People seemed to be everywhere. Ovadyah was glad he had worn his new — his first — black, felt hat, and Ariella was equally gratified at having bought a *sheitel* for the occasion, but both still assumed that the dozen or so people they saw in the lobby were the total number of invited guests. And they had little time to ruminate on any evidence to the contrary because Ovadyah was immediately seized by two yeshivah *bachurim* — rabbinical college students — and led to a room down the hall, while Ariella was similarly, though more gently, waylaid and escorted to the school auditorium, where the wedding ceremony would take place.

In the room to which he was led, Ovadyah was surprised to find several tables laden with food and drink, his father and brothers in their Sunday best, dozens of other men — a good part of the Orthodox population of Hope Heights — and the lion's share of the student body of a nearby rabbinical college. Flabbergasted, he realized that this was the *chassan's tisch*, or "groom's table," the customary men's celebration before the wedding ceremony. He hadn't expected one at all, much less one with so many people present. Everyone began singing spiritedly as he entered and, one by one, they all hugged him. Then everyone sat down and ate, drank and sang — all at once, it seemed to Ovadyah, who just sat there dumbfounded, trying to take it all in. He closed his eyes and was further surprised at the strange emotion welling up from somewhere deep within him, a powerful rush that made the celebration take on the texture of some ancient, tribal rite. He tried to shake the sensation; it wasn't unpleasant, but for some reason it made him nervous.

Ariella's surprise was tempered only by the slight suspicion she had nurtured since the previous day, when Rabbi Solomon's wife had let slip the fact that she had a lot of cooking to do, and Ariella surmised that it might have something to do with their "simple wedding ceremony." It was just like the Solomons to plan a happy surprise like that, she had thought. As she was ushered into the auditorium, any residual doubts she had were instantly dispelled.

In the corner of the auditorium, a three-piece band struck up a loud and lively Jewish wedding song the moment Ariella appeared at the door. Before her was a small sea of women, some she knew and some she didn't, clapping to the music. Before she knew it they were upon her, hugging, kissing, congratulating. Without remembering having sat down, she suddenly found herself in a chair, with circles of dancing women and girls spinning around her, seeming to fly every which way at once. Though she knew just where she was and what was happening, it felt entirely surreal, like some out-of-control daydream. It was as if she were ensconced in some crazy, giant kaleidoscope; the colors of the dancers' dresses blazed in her face and then melted together into a swirling, shimmering blur. Ariella's senses were saturated with the music and movement and she let the feeling wash over her like a warm, soothing wave.

After nearly an hour of revelry, during which Ariella was hoisted, still on her chair, atop several girls' shoulders and regaled with a procession of perfectly executed dance steps performed by pairs of young women, the band suddenly stopped playing. The unexpected vacuum of noise pounded in everyone's ears for the moment it lasted. Then, after shouting, "The *chassan!*" the bandleader, a lively, wiry fellow with an unkempt beard and longish hair, struck up the threesome once again and the group of women parted, clearing a path for the groom.

The double doors opened and the bobbing backs of dancing men appeared. The dancers were clapping in unison, facing the object of their celebration, Ovadyah, who soon appeared at the door himself. He looked down the path at Ariella, seated like a queen, and began a slow march toward her, looking anything but a groom on his third time around with the same bride. Ariella thought he looked positively *frightened*, but he was merely still trying to fathom the emotions that had seized him back at the *chassan's tisch*.

Behind Ovadyah, his entourage danced wildly, egging him on with their singing and clapping. He finally managed a smile and continued moving down the path toward his wife-bride.

Ariella had never seen a *badeken*, or veiling ceremony, before — she had never even been to a religious wedding — yet she was struck with an odd sense of familiarity. Her puzzlement at the feeling expressed itself in a quizzical smile that Ovadyah found powerfully endearing.

As Ovadyah gently lowered Ariella's veil over her face, the music and singing seemed to swell. After gazing for a moment at the veil, and at the smile it softened but could not hide, he turned away and allowed himself to be danced back to the groom's room in preparation for the *chuppah*, or "canopy," the actual wedding service.

Spaceman was freaked. Man, he thought, total weirdness. Everything was so alive, so *charged*. The contact high from the crowd had only gotten stronger and his guitar seemed to play itself. He had felt a buzz in the air when the groom had come in and veiled the lady — and, in yet another strangeness, the dude was a *Puerto Rican* or *Haitian* or something, for crying out loud! He really didn't know what to expect next.

Well, musically he did. It was time for the procession.

The entire crowd had seated itself for the ceremony, the men to one side of the aisle leading to the wedding canopy, the women to the other. The band was to play a medley of slow pieces as the parties walked to the canopy. Spaceman was on the keyboard.

The pieces were easy to perform, which was good since Spaceman only played keyboard occasionally. Even though he had certainly practiced the music enough, he was surprised at how beautiful it sounded that night.

As he played, two young girls came down the aisle, holding hands.

"They're the daughters," Frank broke from his flute for a second and whispered with an almost teary smile.

"*Whose* daughters?" Spaceman whispered back.

"The bride and groom's," Frank said a bit impatiently.

Spaceman missed a note as his face registered incomprehension. Daughters? He thought these were supposed to be religious people!

Next down the aisle came a trio of men: the groom — dressed in a white robe of some sort —

flanked by a stout guy with a reddish beard and a slim, clean-shaven dude. The groom looked nice, Spaceman thought — not just handsome but like the kind of guy you could really talk to and get friendly with. But there was something freaky about him: his face, dark as it was, seemed to *glow*.

As the bride was slowly ushered down the aisle, two women at her side, Spaceman quickly got to work on the finale of the medley. The band really gave it their all and the sweet melody showed their efforts. Spaceman thought the lady was shining even more than the guy was.

Spaceman watched, rapt, as the bride reached the canopy and then started literally walking circles around the groom. When he heard Frank quietly counting the lady's circuits, he half-expected the groom to take off through the roof like a rocket when the count was done. But he didn't.

While the red-bearded guy did some chanting in Hebrew, Spaceman watched the guests. They seemed to be listening to every word, all smiley and teary-eyed.

There was some commotion for a minute or two under the canopy and then the groom murmured something as he placed the ring on the bride's finger. Next, some dude with a big, black beard gave a long speech in what could have been Greek for all Spaceman knew. And the guy read the whole freaking thing from a big piece of *paper* — and occasionally it seemed like he couldn't even read his own handwriting!

When he was done at last, guys started coming up to the canopy, one by one, and each sang a little song — most of them unbelievably off-key. Spaceman looked forward to his next signal from Frank to get the music going again.

Finally, something happened that Spaceman understood. Somebody put a little, velvet pouch on the floor under the canopy and the groom stomped on it as if it were a cockroach. Spaceman knew there was a glass in the bag. He'd seen it in a movie.

Suddenly, Frank kicked him — he'd missed a signal — and he started playing loud and fast. Everyone on the men's side of the room stood up and rushed to the canopy, singing and dancing like crazy. The bride and groom could barely move back down the aisle amid the swelling group of hats and beanies jumping up and down in front of them. As Spaceman played, the contagious joy returned and he found himself jumping up and down just like Frank.

Three hours, a good meal and a lot of playing, smiling and laughing later, Spaceman climbed the stairs to his apartment. He settled himself in an armchair but, contrary to custom, he didn't switch on his television first thing. He wanted to try to hold on to the night's experience as best he could.

CHAPTER 27

Intimate Matters

Ariella hated surgery. She always had, with a visceral loathing impervious to reassurance. And yet here she lay in a hospital bed, counting down the final hours to a serious, lengthy and complex operation. An operation she had *chosen* to have, no less, one she had actually fought for.

It was almost too crazy to believe. But then, she thought, so was so much of life.

Though several weeks had elapsed since the wedding, its multihued memories still wafted through Ariella's mind. She mused over how very much she and Ovadyah had to be thankful for. They were together again, for the first time as a thoroughly Jewish couple; they had actually made it. Ovadyah had landed the job and they had even gone for — and gotten — the house. The place was just right and, most important, they were finally in the thick of Hope Heights' observant community. They were home.

And they had friends as well. Not only friends they had long known about, like Ron and Dina Rosen, but dozens of other friends they had only met at the wedding, men and women whose very presence had been an overture of concern and an offer of camaraderie. It had been a sincere offer, too; there had been no mistaking that in the utter joy of their singing and dancing.

Unfortunately, there had also been lost friends, but Ariella tried not to dwell on that. She and Ovadyah simply had to accept that to some people at Beth Am, they were traitors. They had abandoned ship, those people felt, and for no good reason. Ovadyah had, after all, been much more than a mere congregant. He'd been the *gabbai*, for goodness sake, a major player in synagogue life, and his ethnicity had made him all the more valued, a visible symbol of the congregation's openmindedness. His choice of a Conservative congregation and his enthusiasm and dedication to Judaism had particularly pleased his fellow congregants; it seemed to legitimate their movement. Who could really blame them for hating him, Ariella thought sadly, now that he — and she — had "changed sides"?

There was little open hostility, of course, but the cynicism she had occasionally come up against had been almost palpable. People she and Ovadyah had known and rather liked would pointedly glare at her kerchief or wig and carefully register a smirk or sneer before exchanging pleasantries. And their unmistakably condescending tone barely masked their deep resentment. On several occasions, Ariella had invited a Beth Am family for a Sabbath meal and they would seem to enjoy themselves. Almost invariably, though, some observance at the Gomes home would elicit a comment like "Well, dear, my mother was the daughter of a *rabbi*, and *she* never did it that way." Ariella eventually stopped inviting those people. She had simply wanted to enjoy a festive Sabbath meal with old friends, hoping to maintain their friendships, but she had bitterly come to realize that those relationships would never be the same.

"And how are you feeling today?" an unnaturally chipper nurse suddenly demanded.

How was she feeling? Well, thought Ariella, she was physically ill at the mere thought of being cut by a surgeon's scalpel and thoroughly depressed not only by the length and complexity of the scheduled microsurgery, but by the unlikelihood of a successful reversal of her tubal ligation. She wasn't, she decided, feeling very well at all.

"Oh, just fine."

The nurse smiled doubtfully.

"You look a little apprehensive to me, Ariella."

Well, how'd you like to sit around waiting to be cut open for, oh, several hours so that some near-stranger can play with your insides, she silently responded.

"Surgery's not exactly my favorite pastime," Ariella said blithely, "especially the passive role."

"Ah, well," the nurse replied with a little laugh, "that's part of why I'm here now. The anesthesiologist has approved of your taking these. They will help you relax and feel more at ease."

"These" were two small, pink pills. Ariella hated pills almost as much as surgery.

"Thank you," she lied, taking the medicine and cup of water from the nurse's hands.

"In about an hour, you'll be picked up and taken to surgery."

Whoopee, Ariella thought, summoning a goodbye smile. When that didn't work — the nurse just stood there smiling benevolently — she swallowed the pills. At last, her visitor exited, leaving her alone with her thoughts.

She hadn't had to have this surgery, Ariella told herself again, yet she'd pushed for it like a sumo wrestler. *Why?* What had pushed *her*? She couldn't remember — actually, she couldn't really think very clearly at all — but she knew one thing: she wasn't about to chicken out now.

169

The surgeon had told Ariella that the tests and x-rays had not been encouraging, that she wasn't the best candidate for microsurgery. He'd have to "open her up," as he had put it, to get a better idea whether or not to go ahead with the painstaking and arduous task of reattaching her fallopian tubes.

The television in her room flickered crazily but the jumpy image was unmistakable. The imposing head was scowling and talking in an almost hypnotic cadence. Ariella smiled at the face and then scowled back at it, unimpressed. She had, after all, seen the guy in person. It had been years ago, in a Baptist church in Chicago, and Jesse Jackson had spoken then with the same melodic urgency that the television offered up now in tinny accompaniment to his flickering face.

Suddenly the church was no longer in Chicago but in Ariella's hospital room, having abruptly materialized out of the shimmering, blue aura of the screen. Through a thickening fog, she saw everything again just as it had been two decades earlier: the bodies swaying in the pews, the screaming, chanting, swooning women, the "amens" that filled the reverend's every pointed pause.

As several women appeared to faint to the floor, Ariella once again thought — just as she had back then — how very easy it was to imagine the man precisely as the Chicago locals, white and black alike, perceived him: as a bold and shameless womanizer. He certainly had the female half of the crowd wrapped around his silver tongue, and his readily apparent enjoyment of the histrionics left Ariella nauseous.

Something was talking to her, some other face piercing the fog, but Ariella couldn't focus on it; she was too engrossed in what she saw next in the Baptist church, even though she knew full well that she had seen it there years ago, too.

She was sitting — just as before — in the front pew of the church's balcony, and as the speaker's words grew tiresome, her eyes drifted downward to the thick, polished, wooden railing in front of her. With a start, she realized that the church wasn't a church at all. Etched ornately into the dark walnut was a succession of geometric designs, their maker's intent unmistakable. They were Stars of David.

As Ariella stared at them, the joined pairs of triangles came slowly undone, unbending into vertical lines that moved rapidly across her field of vision. She blinked several times and then it occurred to her that it was she who was moving; the lines had become the pattern on the wallpaper of a long hallway. She was supine on a rolling bed.

Ariella passed a door and caught a word emblazoned in imposing letters above it: "C.A.T." She laughed to herself. The punctuation seemed perfect for so regal and inscrutable a creature. She had always loved cats. In her younger days, she bought anything with a cat motif, cluttering her house with cat prints, cat sculptures, cat ornaments and cat photographs — not to mention several actual cats.

Another surprisingly vivid scene emerged from the strangely fertile fog:

Ariella and Abel had been married just over a year and his Judaism talk had just begun to irritate her. They were living in an apartment underneath Abel's brother's place and the dining room unfolded before her now.

It was Xmastime, and Abel's brother had a magnificently decorated tree in his living room. Abel and Ariella had bought a small tree of their own for their apartment.

Ariella was sitting at the table when Abel called her from the bedroom.

"Look what I found in your cat collection!" he exclaimed, her "cat collection" being a large, cardboard box of feline mementos and assorted junk she hadn't found places for in their small apartment.

Abel walked in from the other room bearing a foot-long, brass lion she vaguely remembered picking up somewhere or other years before. He held it as if it were alive. Ariella noticed something about the lion that hadn't registered when she'd bought it. The animal had a small receptacle of some sort soldered onto its head, and several more along its back. Eight more.

"It's called a menorah," she mumbled.

"I'll be right back!" Abel said abruptly and bolted from the room.

The next thing Ariella knew, Abel had returned to the dining room holding a bag from the grocery store. With a flourish, he reached into it and pulled out a box of small, colored candles. Checking the calendar in the kitchen, he discovered that it was the sixth day of Chanukah. He put candles in six of the receptacles and placed the lit lion on a windowsill. Ariella remembered how the tree had seemed to fade into the background back then, obscured somehow by the tiny blazes dancing atop the colored candles. Now, amid brighter lights and quiet, serious voices that only barely intruded on her vision, the tree disappeared entirely before her mind's eye.

Ariella suddenly started; a sharp pain she couldn't quite place had pierced the fog. She heard an echo of odd, isolated words but could not blend them into coherent thoughts. Some of the words were numbers; she knew that much. Others formed phrases she couldn't fathom. She felt heat in her arm and the fog grew so dense that it seemed to embrace her warmly, like a mother's hug....

Ariella awoke to a vague, throbbing ache and a tsunami of nausea. But then a sudden, incongruous feeling of great calm washed over her, an intuitive conviction that all her hopes had been realized. She still hurt and felt sick, but a deep happiness permeated her soul.

"Ariella? Ariella? Can you hear me? Do you understand what I'm saying?"

The doctor's voice was perfectly clear — and entirely too loud. Ariella understood him but couldn't get her lips to respond. After a moment, she managed to open her eyes and nod.

"Well, Ariella," the surgeon said when he saw her movement, "we did the job."

She was surprised when her mouth gave voice to her thought.

"I know," she said. "I know that."

The doctor looked puzzled at first, and then just smiled at her lingering delirium.

CHAPTER 28

Divergent Paths

Ariella's surgery had taken just over four hours and only one of her fallopian tubes had been repaired — and even it was still twenty percent occluded. There was no assurance that she would ever conceive another child, but now there was at least a possibility.

Ovadyah and the twins were in Ariella's room as she struggled to access reality once again.

"Thank God, it's all over now," Ovadyah whispered in his wife's ear.

"It sure doesn't *feel* like it's over," she moaned with a grimace of discomfort.

Ovadyah smiled, happy to hear Ariella's voice, and a coherent thought to boot.

"Well," he said, "the worst is, anyway."

Ariella moaned again.

The twins came close and kissed her, leaving Ariella frustrated at her inability to respond in kind. Overpowered by nausea, she was using every ounce of her strength just to calm her stomach. Within minutes, she tired and fell asleep.

Hours later, when she was fully awake, the doctor told her what he had told Ovadyah earlier. Ariella wasn't depressed by his cautiously couched words and warnings against unwarranted optimism. All she had wanted in the first place was a *chance* at a child, and now she had it. She had done all she could, and she knew that Judaism required nothing more; God would do whatever He saw fit. A Jew may not rely on a miracle, she knew, but conception now would not require one.

The next day was Friday, and Ovadyah procured wine, candles and challah for the Sabbath. The Bostoner Rebbe, the Chassidic rabbi who had referred them to their surgeon, had arranged accommodations for the family near the hospital as well. Ovadyah was overjoyed that they would have their Shabbos meals together as always. He knew that if anything could transform a cold and uninviting hospital room into a temporary home, Shabbos could.

And it did, though Ariella still couldn't eat anything.

Her recovery began to pick up the next day, however, and though Ovadyah and the twins returned to Hope Heights on Sunday night for work and school the next morning, they made the hour-long drive each evening that week to spend time with Ariella, who grew stronger with each passing day.

Unfortunately, the same could not be said of her roommate, a pale, twentyish woman with long, dark hair, deep, brown eyes and a frailty that was strikingly discordant with her youth. Ariella was ashamed to admit it but she felt better just looking at the newcomer, who seemed not only quite sick but quite frightened.

At first, the two women made simple small talk, exchanging names — hers was Jill — likes, dislikes and hospital gripes. By their second day together, though, they had shared inmatehood long enough for some degree of candor.

"So what're you in for?" Ariella asked, attempting nonchalance.

The fragile young woman hesitated and then quietly responded, "The big `C.'"

Oh, my God, thought Ariella, *the kid's got cancer*.

"Well dear," she said feebly, trying to sound at once compassionate and encouraging, "you've got to muster some real strength for the future."

Then, after a moment's silence, Ariella asked, "What do the medicine men say?"

"That's the problem," Jill murmured.

"What do you mean?"

"They're not saying anything," the girl said in a near whimper. "At least not to me."

Ariella grew pale.

"I know it's not good," Jill continued, finding her voice again, "and I asked how...long it...I..." Ariella took Jill's hand and the physical contact seemed to infuse her demoralized roommate with new energy.

"They don't tell me anything!" she practically shouted. "They're afraid to tell me! And I...I..."

As Jill's anguish streamed from her eyes, suddenly Ariella felt nothing but the other woman's pain. Her mind groped for something appropriate to say but found nothing. The poor thing was facing her own mortality head-on after having lived a mere fraction of a normal life. Platitudes would be demeaning; false hope, downright cruel. There was, quite simply, nothing to say. Instead, Ariella sat up straight — only dimly aware of some slight, nebulous pain — maneuvered herself over to her roommate's bed and held her as she cried.

After a few minutes Jill seemed spent, and Ariella offered what comfort she could summon. She reminded the young woman how doctors like to be cautious, how they prefer pessimism to misleading patients about their prognoses. She recounted cases where even justifiably dire predictions had been frustrated by unforeseen changes for the better. And she assured Jill that she would be in her prayers.

"I'm an Orthodox Jew," she said, "and I believe with all my heart that my prayers make a difference. They may not make *the* difference — God has His own plans — but they do make *a* difference. And I'll be praying for you."

Jill appreciated Ariella's concern and quietly, earnestly thanked her.

Ariella couldn't help but regard her roommate as bearing a message of sorts, a sign. Here she herself sat, recovering quite nicely, all things said and done, from surgery to enable her to conceive a child — *another* child — at forty, feeling like Sisyphus. And not three feet from her lay an anguished, moribund youth who'd probably sell her soul for even the most mundane, childless future.

By the time Ariella was discharged from the hospital, she thought her new friend looked worse than when she had arrived. She hoped she was wrong.

Although Ariella couldn't wait to get out of the place, she surveyed the hospital room one last time to make sure she hadn't forgotten anything. She wanted to remove every vestige of her stay there, as if anything left behind might somehow hold part of her soul back along with it. Her gaze drifted to Jill, and she knew the time had come to say goodbye.

Jill managed a faint smile and held out her hands. Ariella took them in her own and, while Ovadyah stood in the lobby, puzzling over his wife's extended delay, the two women eight floors above him embraced and cried for a long, long time before the overlap of their lives drew to a close and each went her separate way.

CHAPTER 29

Outrageous Fortune

A riella hung up just as her husband walked in the front door. One look at the expression on her face told Ovadyah that she was upset.

"Who were you talking to?" he asked with concern.

"Fertility Specialist Associates," Ariella replied in an exaggeratedly whiny and nasal receptionist's voice. "How may I help you?"

"Any luck with an appointment yet?"

"Actually, yes…if you call that lucky."

It had been a difficult year-and-a-half. Though Ariella had known all along that she and Ovadyah might never conceive another child, their failure to do so had sunk her into a deep funk. She had found herself repeatedly swallowing sorrow, frustration, self-pity and at times even anger — though at no one in particular.

In recent weeks, however, a certain solace had set in, an unexpected calm that had made her reconsider her plight. Maybe she and Ovadyah simply weren't meant to have another child. She had always *known*, intellectually, that "God knows best," but over the weeks, she had come to *realize* it — and its implications — more fully.

Nonetheless, they had decided on one last try. Should it fail, they would accept their fate without question, satisfied that they had at least made every reasonable effort. As they had learned, the importance of doing all one can — known in Hebrew as *hishtadlus*, or "effort" — was a fundamental principle of Judaism, no less than ultimate acceptance of God's will.

The phone call had been the first act of Ariella's final hishtadlus in the matter. It had taken weeks of such calls to wheedle her way into a respected fertility clinic in Boston — she wasn't considered a good candidate for treatment — and now, strangely enough, ambivalence clouded her triumph. She wondered if she had perhaps gone beyond *hishtadlus* in her obsessive pursuit of another child.

"Hey, listen," Ovadyah said, "if you don't want to pursue things any further, you know that's fine with me."

"I know."

"Maybe it's just not worth all the procedures and tension and pain."

"Maybe."

Ovadyah took his wife's hand and she looked up at him.

"I just don't know," she said finally. "If this turns out to be a dead end, then I really will accept things. But I just feel I should keep this appointment, no matter how much part of me doesn't want to. I'm going to force myself to go, and that's that."

Ovadyah recognized a tone of voice he dared argue with only at considerable risk.

"When's the appointment?" he asked resignedly.

"A week from today."

A week of seconds ticked away and another Wednesday morning arrived as expected. Ariella had until the early afternoon to decide whether to actually keep her appointment. Her indecision had become an emotional thumbscrew, tormenting her as never before. Yet, having persevered through his own disappointments over the years, Ovadyah had unwittingly taught her equanimity. It was imperative, she told herself, that she maintain a positive attitude through it all.

Once the twins were off to school and Ovadyah had left for work, Ariella phoned her office to say she wouldn't be in that day. Whatever her decision, she figured, she needed time to herself.

Ariella thought back over the previous day's events, about the idea that had dawned when she'd awoke, about the way she had felt all morning at work, about the afternoon's sudden thunderstorm and how wet she had gotten when she'd stopped at the drugstore on the way home. Today, though, she had nowhere to go, at least for the time being, so she spent a few hours doing housework, reading the newspaper and listening to some classical music. When she could no longer deny that the morning had disappeared, she forced herself to eat a late lunch.

A half-hour before she would have to leave the house to make her appointment, she entered the bedroom to check the previous day's drugstore purchase. Within seconds, she was on the phone. "Fertility Specialist Associates," whined the receptionist. "How may I help you?"

"This is Ariella Gomes," she said hurriedly, flustered with excitement. "I'd like to cancel my four o'clock appointment."

"Certainly," came the nasal reply. "May I ask the reason for the cancellation?"

Ariella took a deep breath.

"Pregnancy," she said.

CHAPTER 30

Critical Issue

One never knows, Rabbi Sofer thought, when a child will pose a question with deep implications for his or her life. It was one of teaching's — and parenting's — greatest challenges to be constantly on the lookout for such opportunities, and to be primed with just the right words to plant the most suitable seeds in a child's incredibly fertile mind.

Toweling his six-year-old daughter off after her bath, Rabbi Sofer was sure he recognized harbingers of just such an opportunity.

They had returned only an hour earlier from the Hope Heights Hebrew Day School Chanukah program. One of the evening's highlights had been a medley of Jewish songs sung by his daughter's class, with several parents providing accompaniment on various instruments. Ovadyah Gomes, the proud father of a recently arrived third daughter, had played the flute, and played it beautifully.

Rabbi Sofer, a teacher at Hope Heights Hebrew, could almost see the question forming in his little girl's furrowed brow; she seemed both anxious and hesitant. Knowing that she had always been a thoughtful, perceptive kid, he wondered what was going through her mind.

"Abba?" the little face peering out from the folds of terry-cloth finally asked, testing the conversational waters.

"Yeeeessss?" her father responded exaggeratedly, as was his playful custom at times.

"Abba, you know Ruth and Daphna's daddy?"

Uh oh, thought Rabbi Sofer, *here it comes*.

"Sure I know him," he replied with carefully crafted nonchalance. "Didn't he play well tonight?"

"Sure did!" the child agreed, momentarily derailed from her original concern.

Rabbi Sofer had often wondered how the kids in the school, and his own kids in particular, viewed Ovadyah. The Gomes girls, he knew, were fully accepted at Hope Heights Hebrew, and stood out only for being twins. But then, their skin was no darker than that of many Jews of Sephardic or Middle Eastern ancestry. Unlike their father, they didn't look different from their peers. How, he had mused on many occasions, did the kids regard "Ruth and Daphna's daddy"?

As it happened, Rabbi and Mrs. Sofer had gotten to know Ovadyah and Ariella Gomes quite well over the past year or so, ever since the couple's "surprise" wedding. They had even asked the Gomeses if they thought other Jewish families might be reluctant to marry into theirs because Ovadyah was a convert and a "person of color" to boot. The Sofers had been impressed with their friends' realistic yet positive attitude.

"It's one thing to recognize someone who looks different from you as a full Jew," Ovadyah had explained, "and even to love him as one, but even the remotest possibility of *shvartze* grandchildren is still a bit much for a lot of Jews to handle."

"Look," Ariella had chimed in, "Jews carry a lot of baggage around, especially American Jews. There's a good deal of old-fashioned bigotry among us, too. That's life. But it's not the end of the world."

"Do you really think it's any different among darker-skinned people?" Ovadyah had added. "You wouldn't believe the disdain and even hatred I've seen among the brown, the browner and the brownest people. I've met Hispanics, South Americans and even blacks with virtual Klan mentalities when it came to anyone darker than themselves!"

"Listen," Ariella had concluded, "the truth is that, in a way, we're really blessed. We have the perfect litmus test for a prospective son-in-law. Anybody who would shy away from our family is simply not for our family in the first place. Some people make demands regarding their son-in-law's profession or place of residence. Well, one of the things we demand is, I guess, sort of built into the system!"

Rabbi Sofer thought back on that conversation while anticipating his daughter's question. He knew what *he* would say if a *shidduch*, or "match," were proposed between one of *his* children and one of the Gomeses'. But what was his child's perception? How would she even phrase the question?

"But Abba," came the little voice from within the towel, "their daddy, is he...I mean, is he..."

"Yes?" Rabbi Sofer gently coached.

Finally, out it came. The child finally found the words she had been seeking.

"Is he a MISTER?" she blurted out in an earnest, curious burst of syllables. "Or is he a RABBI?" Rabbi Sofer laughed heartily and happily in his soul.

"Well," he answered, "I don't think he's a rabbi, dear, though he certainly learns Torah whenever he can — probably more than some rabbis do. So I guess you'd have to call him a mister, just a plain Jew.

"Just a plain Jew," he repeated to himself as much as to his daughter, "like any other."

Glossary

AMIDAH — main, silent portion of the Jewish prayer service

ASHKENAZIM — Jews of Eastern European extraction [adj.: ASHKENAZIC]

BAALEI TESHUVAH — "returnees" to Jewish tradition

BADEKEN — "veiling" of a bride's face prior to her marriage

BARUCH HASHEM — Thank God

BEIN HASHEMASHOT — twilight

BEIS DIN/BEIT DIN — Jewish court

BENTCHER — book containing the grace after meals and Jewish songs

CHALLAH — braided bread eaten on the Sabbath

CHASSAN — groom

CHAVRUSAH — Torah study partner

CHAVURAH(OT) — study group

CHESSED — kindness

CHUMASH — Bible

CHUPPAH — wedding canopy

DAVEN — pray

FRUM — observant of Jewish law

GABBAI — synagogue sexton

GADOL — [lit.: "great one"] Jewish scholar/religious leader

GEIRUS — conversion

GER — convert to Judaism

GET — Jewish divorce document

GOYIM — [lit.: "nations"] non-Jews

GUT YOMTOV — "Happy holiday"

HAGGADAH — account of the exodus from Egypt, read on Passover

HALACHAH — Jewish law

HATAFAT DAM BRIT — symbolic incision reenacting circumcision [also: HATAFAH]

HISHTADLUS — effort necessary to effect a result

KABBALAT HAMITZVOT — acceptance of Divine commandments

KASHERING — rendering kitchen implements kosher

KEFITZAS HADERECH — miraculous shortening of a trip

KICHEL — a hard, cookie-like snack

KIDDUSH — [lit.: "sanctification"] Sabbath prayer chanted over wine

KITZUR — colloquial shortening of the title of a popular work on daily Jewish laws

KLAL YISRAEL — the Jewish people

MAMZER(IM) — child born of a forbidden union; such a child may not marry most Jews [fem.: MAMZERES(OS)]

MAMZERUS — status of a MAMZER

MATZO — unleavened bread eaten on Passover

MECHITZAH — partition separating men from women in synagogue

MENORAH — candelabrum used for Chanukah candles

MESHUGA — crazy

MIKVAH — ritual bath

MINYAN — quorum of ten men necessary for certain parts of synagogue service

MITZVAH(OT/OS) — Divine commandments

MOHEL — ritual circumcisor
NIDDAH — menstruant
NIDDUS — menstruation
NUSACH — "style" of Jewish prayer
REBBE — teacher of Torah
ROSH HASHANAH — Jewish New Year
ROSH YESHIVAH — dean of a rabbinical college
SEDER — festive commemoration of the exodus from Egypt, conducted on Passover
SEPHARDIM — Jews of Iberian, North African or Middle Eastern extraction [adj.: SEPHARDIC]
SHAATNEZ — Biblically forbidden mixture of wool and linen in garment
SHABBAT/SHABBOS — Sabbath
SHALOM ALEICHEM — [lit.: "peace unto you"] Jewish greeting
SHEITEL — wig worn by Orthodox married woman
SHEMA — fundamental Jewish declaration of God's existence and unity
SHIUR — class on a Torah topic
SHUL — synagogue
SHVARTZE — black
SIDDUR — prayer book
SIMCHAT TORAH — Jewish holiday celebrating the completion of the yearly cycle of Torah readings
SUKKAH — temporary dwelling inhabited on SUKKOT
SUKKOT — holiday commemorating the Israelites' travels through the wilderness
TALMUD — fundamental, authoritative work of Jewish law and lore
TEFILLIN — phylacteries worn by Jewish men during weekday morning prayers
TEVILAH — immersion in a MIKVAH
TICHEL — kerchief
TISCH — [lit.: "table"] festive gathering
TORAH — Jewish Bible and Oral Law
TREIF — non-kosher
TZITZIS — fringes affixed to four-cornered garments worn by Jewish men
YESHIVAH — rabbinical college

Printed in Great Britain
by Amazon

24215085R00106